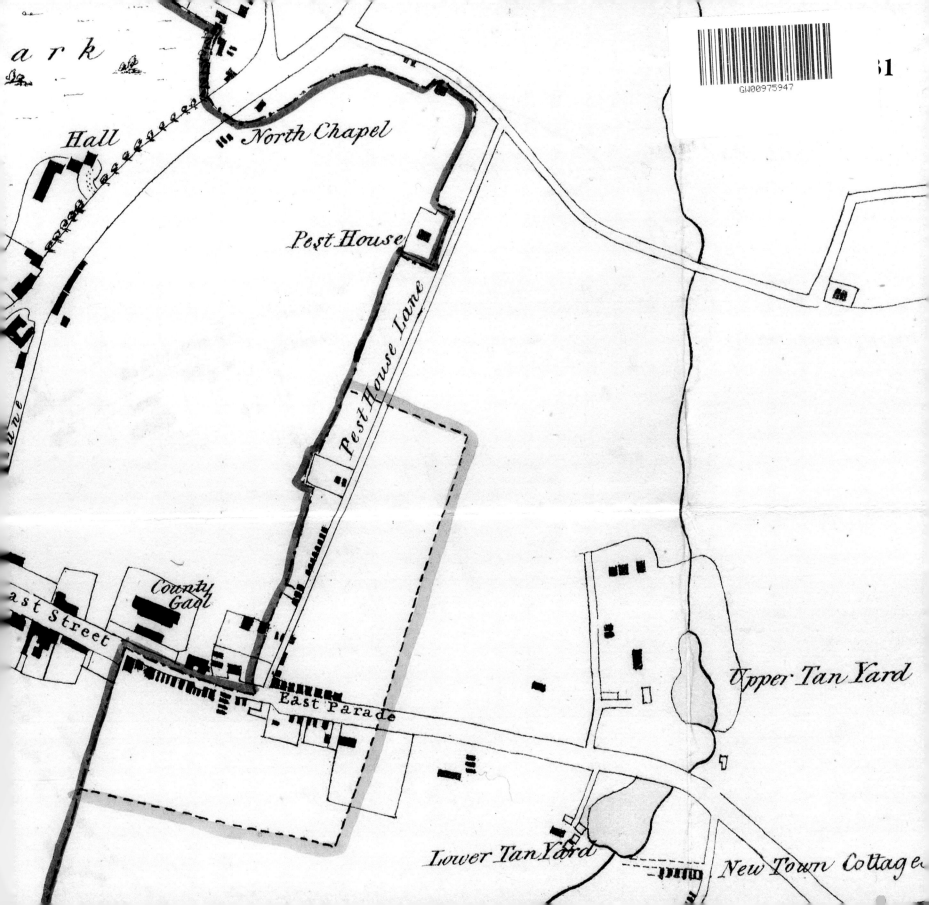

31

a r k

Hall

North Chapel

Pest House

Pest House Lane

County Gaol

East Street

East Parade

Upper Tan Yard

Lower Tan Yard

New Town Cottages

Horsham Houses Revisited

By Dr Annabelle Hughes

Horsham Museum Society
2016

Cover and format designed by Horsham Museum and Horsham District Council
Published by Horsham Museum Society for Horsham Museum/ Horsham District Council

ISBN 978-1-902484-63-1

A CIP catalogue record for this work is available from the British Library

Contents

Foreword

Realising in 2015 that 2016 would be the 30th anniversary of Dr Annabelle Hughes' seminal work on *Horsham houses* led me to ask Annabelle if she would be willing to re-write the text to include a wealth of information that she has discovered and to raise funds for the Museum, for which she is a long-time supporter and advocate. At least once a month, Annabelle would pop in to the museum excitedly talking about a new piece of research, adding to the very rich and multi-faceted history of the town's buildings. Annabelle was delighted to be offered the chance, whilst the Friends of Horsham Museum were pleased to publish it, to help raise funds for the museum.

Over the next six months Annabelle worked on the text and selected images that she wanted to use to tell the story. The original publication was produced in the pre-digital age, now with the changes in print technology and availability of images the museum had the opportunity to greatly add to the visual record of the town. To bring the story up to date, Rooney & Co (who have supported this project from the beginning) have also provided colour photographs taken in 2016, adding a contemporary view of the town's old buildings.

What was originally a straightforward publication became a multi-faceted work that took advantage of the Museum's superb photographic and art collection, modern photographs by Rooney & Co, and thanks to the generosity of Glyn Martin, some delightful delicate sketches of the town along with a fully revised text. Julie Poole, Horsham Museum's Assistant Curator who had skilfully edited and crafted the publication *Reminiscences of Horsham,* the centenary edition of Henry Burstow's memories, took on the challenge of blending these elements to create a new work – and Kerrie Braham had the daunting task of designing a modern book that does justice to the subject. It has been a long process that has involved a great deal of thought, ensuring that design did not take over substance and image does not conflict with text.

The book *Horsham Houses Revisited* is a visual and stimulating treat that does justice to the town of Horsham. It will be a reference work for future generations as well as an inspiration to those that love the town. I trust that it fully repays the commitment to the town by those who have fought hard to preserve the historical elements, whilst knowing that it cannot be kept in aspic. The book is a modern take on an old subject and more than fulfils the expectation of it when first suggested back in September 2015.

Jeremy Knight
Curator, Museum and Heritage Manager
Horsham Museum and Art Gallery

Rooney & Co. are delighted to support this publication. We have been estate agents working in Horsham and the surrounding community for over 30 years, and seen a growing interest in the historic houses of Horsham. The book *Horsham Houses* by Annabelle Hughes, published in 1986, has been on the desk of our agency and is frequently consulted as we engage with clients over the fascinating heritage of the town. At a personal level, I have my own copy, and have taken great pleasure in the fact that I have lived in one of the homes featured in Annabelle's first book. We were delighted to be able to offer the services of our estate photographer to add recent images of the town for this publication – I hope you will get as much enjoyment out of this book as I have, and I am delighted to be able to publicly thank Annabelle Hughes for her years of research in Horsham's houses, which has culminated in this work.

Duncan Rooney
Rooney & Co estate agents

Acknowledgements

Horsham Houses Revisited

It was nearly thirty years ago, that on the back of work on timber-framed buildings for my doctoral thesis and in anticipation of large-scale developments pending in Horsham, I was spurred on to investigate every early building in Horsham that I could get into, and set out my findings for the public. My hope was that this would raise awareness and feed into any planning process, and since the debacle of Bournes (its site is now under Boots the chemist) we have not completely lost another early building, although it has sometimes been a close thing.

My declared intent was 'to show how much a study of merely one aspect of Horsham – its early buildings, with documentary support – can contribute to a better understanding of the whole'. As many will know, I haven't stopped exploring buildings, and apart from 13/15 East Street, a drawing of which was shoe-horned in as 'a recent discovery' in 1986, there have been other exciting finds, such as more about the 8-bay building along the south side of East Street, enough significant timber to confirm the original appearance and age of the Red Lion (on the Waterstones corner site) an earlier core in the King's Head with clues to its raised roof level and hints of painted decoration, and a further part of the range along Colletts Alley.

There have also been some unhappy moments; none more so than when fine details disappeared or were unnecessarily removed during 'renovation' of the property that was once the gaoler's house, next to the North Walk corner site. To balance that has been the restoration of 13/15 East Street (Stan's Way) which finally settled on which side the early 'hall' was sited (east), and revelations about land ownership while exploring the documentary background of some of the Causeway houses in greater depth, not to mention some fascinating 'dendro-dates'.

Coming to buildings as an historian, I cannot separate the background revealed in documents from historical structures that survive; I believe these complement each other and provide a more rounded picture. So it was that in 1986 the first part of Horsham Houses consisted of 'The making of medieval Horsham', as well as a basic introduction to structure, and these have now been recast, in view of my on-going studies of documents.

My earlier acknowledgements still stand, and I must repeat my debts to Sylvia Bright and my family (I still don't have a dining room), and add members, past and present, of the Wealden Buildings Study Group, Jeremy Knight at Horsham Museum, and staff, past and present, at the West Sussex Record Office, not forgetting the owners and occupants of the buildings.

Giovanni Battista Ferraro's *Cavallo Frenato* ['The Bridled Horse'] (1602). Control of horses often portrayed wealth, power and status. This book was bought by the Friends of Horsham Museum to reflect the interest that Horsham's William Albery had in Lorinery. [MS 2011.259]

Chapter One
The Making of Medieval Horsham

Horsham's arrival on the map and its continued success over centuries has depended on two activities: marketing and administration. Both those activities have been particularly successful because of Horsham's geography; that is, where it is in relation to the coast, to a river, to the Weald and to London.

Hundreds of years before the Normans arrived in force, the inhabitants of the fertile coastal plain of Sussex were in the habit of driving their animals north into the woodlands of the Weald in spring and summer, to take advantage of extra pasturage and exploit its natural resources. They tracked along the river valleys, trod the Roman ways, found good crossing points and fords, and made clearings for summer enclosures and shelters. Some began to stay on and over-winter, particularly if they were too poor to hold land on the coast; building more permanent shelters, clearing for cultivation (assarting) or re-opening ancient clearings. They set up breeding stock – of horses in particular – to serve the needs of travellers, and most of the coastal manors maintained their links with 'outliers' in the Weald by continuing to collect tithes (church tax) and rents from them.

Horsham was on one of those northward tracks, at a good river crossing, and Saxon charters tell us it was valued as wood and swine pastures from at least the second half of the 900s. It must also have had a special appeal for horse breeders and traders, for its name – Horsham – has remained unchanged since then. It was not far from the well-drained greensand belt of the Forest of St Leonard, to where horses could be moved in winter, so that although they were still near the point of sale and exchange, they were saved from being bogged down in the heavy mud close to the Arun.

These breeders and traders and their families must have exploited their role in the transport business by bartering and selling other goods and services with their customers. Their success attracted other settlers with different skills, and it is possible that before long, a local thegn provided a wooden chapel, staffed with a man of his own choice, on the north bank of the river, near the ford.

Watercolour of Chesworth House, unsigned; c.1850-1880.

We know the names of at least three of Horsham's Saxon landowners in the tenth century (900s). Ealderman Aethelwold who was succeeded by his brother Eadric, when Horsham was still part of the huge manor of Washington, and 'Ceoldred', whose name survives on one of Horsham's most historic sites – Chesworth – which derives from Ceoldred's 'worth' or farm. Ceoldred or his successors may have provided the first chapel. The place-name 'Roffey' is also Saxon in origin, and shows how north Horsham was already being used before the Normans came; 'rogh' (deer) and 'hay' (netting) described an area where game was driven for hunting.

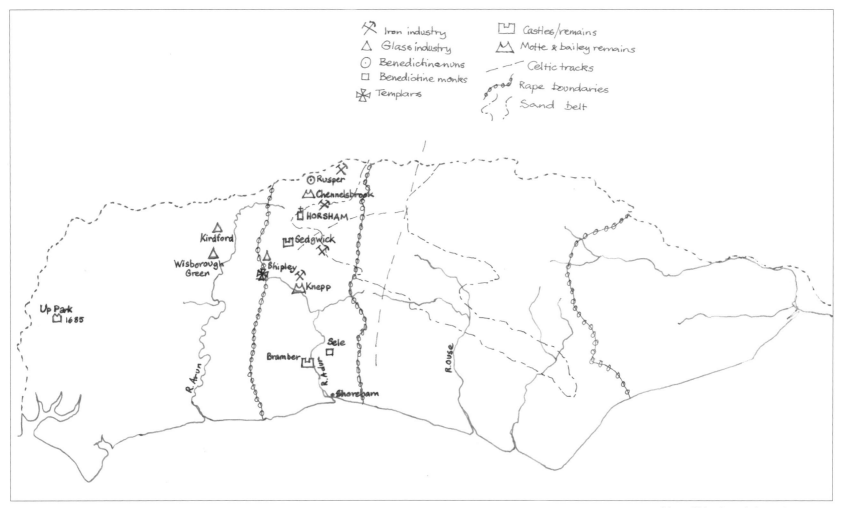

Map of Horsham in its early context.

After 1066, as William of Normandy began to consolidate his hold on England, it was of particular importance to secure the south coast against other invaders, and to keep the local people passive. Using existing boundaries, he carved up the area that is now largely Sussex into five castellanies – a lordship depending upon a castle – each extending from the coast into the woodland or Weald, and put them under the command of some of his most trusted followers. Each castellany or 'rape' was based on a castle and a port, and sported a chain of fortified mounds or castles along its north-south line of communication. William de Braose established the principal castle of his rape at Bramber and the Domesday survey of 1086 credits him with some 325 estates throughout the south and west. Bramber Castle was easily accessible by boat from his newly planted port at Shoreham, and was linked with further outposts at Knepp, Sedgwick and Chennelsbrook. It seems too much of a coincidence that these three fortified sites were all within a seven-mile radius of Horsham – the normal radius for a medieval market was about six and a half miles, to allow for the journey there and back and trading in between, all in one day.

Two Doomsday entries: the one as in the original (above), the other a translation (below).

The Land of William de Braiose
In Burbece Hundred

William de Braiose holds Beddinges. King Edward held it in his farm. It then vouched for 32 hides. It has not paid geld. Of these hides William de Warren has 10 hides in his rape. William de Braiose holds the others. There is land for 28 ploughs. In demesne are 4 ploughs and 62 villeins, and 48 bordars with 24 ploughs. There are 2 churches, and 6 acres of meadow. Wood for 70 hogs, and 20 hogs for rent, and 2 sextaries of honey.

In the great survey of 1086 the settlement of Horsham is 'hidden' within the entry for the estate of Washington, but nine households with 1½ plough teams (12 oxen) and a small herd of pigs are separately listed under lands belonging to the Archbishop (of Canterbury) which lay to the west of the present town. Later, this became known as Marlpost. King Aethelstan, the first king of all England (927-39) granted the estate of West Tarring to Canterbury before he died, and Marlpost was part of that estate. The gift was confirmed by Athelstan's brother and successor, Edmund (939-46).

It seems that not only travellers were making use of what Horsham had to offer in the way of provisions and services. Those pioneers who settled in the Weald and began to cultivate the wilderness could be sure of being able to buy necessities at the start of their labours, and of finding a ready market when they had something to sell. It was probably William de Braose's son, Philip, who recognised the success and further potential of Horsham in about 1140, when he built a substantial stone church to meet the needs of the growing community, parts of which survive in the present building. Parishes in the Weald tended to be created later than those south of the spring line of the Downs, and were imposed upon an earlier pattern of land ownership. Formally or by custom, estates to the south continued to exploit the seasonal resources of the Weald, and over time, claimed those 'outliers' as their own. Two charters of the 900s show that this process – and Horsham's place in it – was already well-established.

947
I Eadred, king of the English [946-55]... grant to a certain very faithful and beloved thegn of mine named Eadric... twenty hides in that place [called] Washington...These are the wood-pastures which belong thereto, Wynburh's spear, and the three Crockhursts and Horsham, Yffel's clearing and Hazelwick and Gotwick...

963
I Edgar [958-975] king of all Britain have granted a certain piece of land in... Washington to a certain bishop [called] Aethelwold [Winchester 963-88]... These are its swine pastures, firstly Wynburh's spear, then west Crockhurst, then another Crockhurst, then the third Crockhurst, Then Horsham, then Yffel's clearing and Hazelwick and Gotwick...

As seasonal populations settled and increased, so these 'outliers' broke away and formed new parishes and estates that contained a patchwork of older administrations. Horsham included parts of at least five estates or manors, and as late as the 1400s was still paying some dues to Washington. So out of the staging post had grown a bustling, and thriving, market centre.

In 1201, the great-grandson of the de Braose of Domesday, another William, was granted a charter by King John, giving him freedom from royal interference in all his lands. To capitalise on this, and probably in response to local pressure from prosperous tenants who wanted more say in their own affairs, he followed the prevailing fashion of the time, and granted Horsham corporate rights as a borough. In essence, this established legally that the inhabitants of a defined place could pay a fixed annual rent to their landlord instead of providing labouring services, and so became a corporate body running their own affairs. In practice this was already happening in a number of places where the rents and market dues were worth more to a landowner than the labours of his tenants, but formal recognition of such status was much sought after. This must have been so in Horsham, for by 1235 an official legal record gives it borough status.

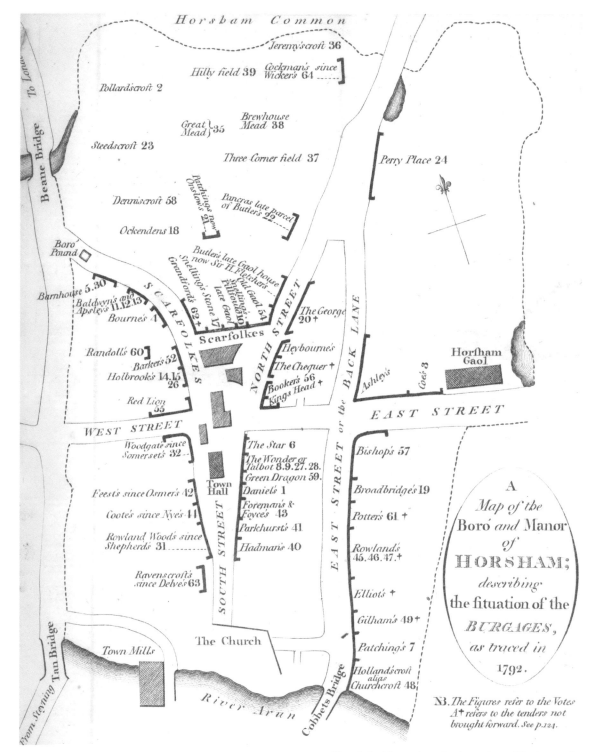

The dotted lines show the boundary of the borough, and the main N/S routes in Medieval Horsham.

Hedger's Blacksmiths, London Road, Horsham, c. 1911.

From later records it is clear that regular borough courts were held in the town – the *Court Baron*, which dealt with matters concerning the ancient customs of the manor and its tenants, the rights of the lord and the privileges of the tenants; the *Court Leet*, which was concerned with the local administration of the borough and dealing with both civil and criminal cases; the *Portmot* or *Portmoot* which met every three weeks to deal with cases of debt and trespass under 40 shillings. The first two courts were usually presided over by the lord's steward, the latter by locally elected officials. These officials, chosen from nominations made at the Courts Baron and Leet, which were often held together, consisted of one or two bailiffs, two or three constables, a jury of between 13 and 23 burgesses, five head-boroughs responsible for the several streets, ale tasters, leather searchers and sealers responsible for the measures, weights and quality of market goods, and a town crier. One or more of these officials is named in surviving records from as early as 1288. A borough was not only the centre of exchange for surrounding settlements, but also where people could send their sons to serve apprenticeships to craftsmen and traders. From names in early documents from the 1200s, it is clear there was a wide range of such men in and around Horsham – blacksmiths, coopers, drapers, hurdle and basket-makers, locksmiths, turners, fullers and tailors to mention only a few.

Façade of P.A. Rooney & Co. in their original location Queen Street, Horsham. In 1985, the earlier shop sign for 'C.F.Lansly General Draper, Hosier & Outfitter' was still in situ.

Watercolour painting attributed to Thomas Mann: 'Morth's Gardens looking towards Causeway', 1871-1890. Some believe this to be Pump Alley; however, this is due to Morth's Gardens having moved along the Causeway slightly, when the house was rebuilt.

It was at this time that the market area must have been officially paced out and the sites of the burgage plots established. These were the 52 plots whose owners paid the corporation's rent of a shilling per annum to de Braose and his successors, and who were foremost in the commercial life of the town and responsible for its administration. From the beginning in Horsham, these privileges were attached to sites, whether open ground or built upon, and not to people or buildings. Quite reasonably most of the burgage sites were around the market-place, possibly chosen because it was the nearest large level space to the river crossing, with footpath access to the church. It covered all that area now called the Carfax and Market Square, as far down as the line of Morth Gardens – a huge triangle funnelling down to the parish church, which then would have functioned as meeting hall, legal centre and a focus for social activities as well as a place of worship. Curiously there were several burgage sites away from this area which seemed to remain under-developed for centuries – crofts north of the Carfax and east of an old trackway from the river (Denne Road) and north of the Carfax (towards Horsham Park). It is possible that these were the remnants of early common fields, which had been originally cultivated in strips, but this is an enduring puzzle.

What had once been a rather ad hoc business of barter and exchange, functioning on word-of-mouth recommendations and relying chiefly on the travellers compelled through Horsham by the terrain, now developed into an organised economy, with well-policed markets taking place on one or two days each week. Then the place would seethe with villagers and their produce, animals for sale and slaughter, pedlars of small wares who wandered from market to market, and the inhabitants making capital out of their week's work.

Craftsmen and traders alike operated from the front of their houses, in a room open onto the market-place, where those who had travelled in to buy and sell drew up their loaded wagons and carts. As the markets became more established and prosperous, local residents erected collapsible counters on their frontages and travelling traders put up stalls – for which they would have been charged a ground rent. There were regulations governing the times when these stalls could be put up, and when they had to be dismantled – and traders would be fined for trying to gain an advantage by 'fore-stalling'. Rents were charged to regular stall-holders, and the quality of staple goods such as bread and ale maintained by local laws, and national legislation, upheld at the manorial and borough courts. The price of bread fluctuated with the price of corn, which was fixed by magistrates after Michaelmas (September) each year, according to the harvest.

Less than thirty years after Horsham had become a borough, the town was such a success that in 1233 the de Braose of the time acquired a grant for an annual fair, which ran for between three days and a week. This could attract people from 20 miles distance, or even further, and most of the visitors would stay for at least one night, probably paying about a half-penny for a bed in one of the residents' houses. Tolls were taken on any goods brought in and about three pence a day charged for a stall. A proportion of this income went to the lord of the manor, the rest into the borough coffers.

'Take-away' food would have been a feature of a fair, in the shape of hot pies and spit-roasted meats, washed down with weak ale. Ordinary villagers could rub shoulders with wealthy landowners and merchants, even with representatives of the royal household come to buy provisions for the not-too-distant 'hunting lodges' at Knepp and Holbrook.

'Cultivation of Grain in use amongst the Peasants, and the Manufacture of Barley and Oat Bread' from *The Arts in the Middle Ages and The Period of the Renaissance* by Paul Lacroix (1874).

Hunting attire, from *Strutt's Complete View of the Press and Habits of the People of England* (1852). [MS 2008.316.2]

The town officials were kept constantly on the move, checking weights and measures, collecting dues, hearing complaints and patrolling the fairground at night, after curfew. Some fairs operated their own courts to try any cases that arose in the duration – Horsham people would have been quite familiar with such proceedings from their own regular borough courts.

The assizes at Chichester included several Horsham cases during this period: a wife and her lover killed her husband and fled – they were outlawed; a man killed his brother in a fight; two leading inhabitants were fined for selling wine and cloth against regulations – human nature was not very different, even then! One of the earliest lists of Horsham men is of those summoned to the Chichester assizes of 1288 to serve as jurors.

Horsham men as jurors at the 1288 assizes

Robert le Frounceys (bailiff)   *Richard le Turner*
Walter Randolph   *Richard Chanterel*
Ralph de Stannestrete   *Godfrey Hauthemer*
Robert le Clerk   *Ralph de Laffield*
Gilbert de la Bure   *Richard de la Grace*
Walter Burgeys   *John de Hamelhurst*
Richard le Marescal

In 1295 a summons was sent to the burgesses of Horsham to send two representatives to the king's parliament at Westminster; the first time this had happened and as a result of the barons' rebellion against Henry III. At first this was seen as a privilege, but later as an onerous duty to be avoided if possible, for the men might have to leave their own businesses at in inconvenient time of year and the town was expected to pay their expenses. On the other hand, it could be an opportunity for an aspiring local entrepreneur or landowner to make important contacts in a wider sphere of influence; a jumping-off point that could lead to greater things.

Not all those chosen to represent Horsham were as respectable as one might have thought; one of the first two, Walter Randolf, had been one of those selling against the assize. We know that he owned at least four houses, a mill and 3 acres, and land elsewhere in the county, and a burgage called Randoll's or Randolfes was recorded on the west side of the Carfax as late as 1598. The other man chosen, Walter Burgess, was the founder of the first chantry chapel at the parish church, 13 years' later in 1307. When Burgess died in 1325, he owned property in Horsham parish worth over £10, as well as in Warnham, Rusper, Slinfold and Ifield. Of his three daughters, Maud married a Shoreham man, and Alice a man from Winchelsea. Among the endowments of that first chantry foundation is the earliest known reference to a commercial

premises in the town – a shop, rented for 4d, by Alan Dragon. In 1296 an Adam Dragon paid the national tax under 'Rozghee' (Roffey).

Before 1300, the wealth of Horsham can be judged by a very obvious piece of evidence – the parish church. By about 1250, the Norman church had been almost completely replaced by a fine Early English building, and a little later a tall shingled spire was added that would have been visible from nearly every direction.

Parish Church; Ray Luff, 1988.

Normandy.

East end of the churchyard and weather-boarded cottages adjacent to medieval Priests' House.

Drawing of the old Priest's House (now demolished) at the east end of St Mary's Parish Church, 1885.

We know that it was served by at least four clergy, and the natural way for both a community and individuals to demonstrate success was to put money into the most prestigious local building. Townspeople of substance left money for yearly masses and prayers or 'obits' for their souls, but the endowment of a chantry (chapel or extra altar) with a salaried priest was beyond the means of most. In Horsham two such chantries were founded – in 1307 and 1447 – each with considerable endowments in lands and rents. The signatories and witnesses were men high on the taxation lists, and who represented Horsham at parliaments, or came from families that did so. Moreover, in 1457, a parish guild or 'brotherhood' was established as a kind of co-operative chantry for those who were not rich enough to pay for their own, and it also supported a small house for the really destitute, near the east end of the church, in the Normandy. Photographs of this building and of an adjoining 'priests' house' (perhaps associated with one or other of the chantries) have been identified.

Watercolour painting of a timber clad house with a steep, stone roof: the Priest's House near St Mary's Parish Church; 1850-1890.

Normandy, east end of the churchyard. After demolition of the Priests' House, the weatherboarding was removed to reveal close-studding on adjacent cottages, very similar to the front of Bishops in Denne Road.

We know that by the early 1400s there was a beautifully carved chancel screen painted with the twelve apostles, surmounted by a beam carrying a rood – a crucifixion scene with figures – and in the choir was a painting or 'pieta' statue – the Virgin with the body of her Son in her arms. The painted wooden ceiling and angel figures may have originated at this time, although they were later restored and re-touched.

Ranworth rood screen: what Horsham screen must have looked like.

Restored Corbel Angels.

The lists of named tax-payers that follow are presented in order of wealth calculated on their borough possessions – several owned property elsewhere. About 30% of the population were below the tax threshold. Note the recurring family names, and those that give a clue to the man's calling or are descriptive. Also note how influence became concentrated in fewer hands over the years. An asterisk indicates that a man represented the borough at least once at a parliament, and underlined are the few women taxpayers, several of them widows (relicta).

1296 (42) BOROUGH	1327 (36) BOROUGH	1332 (26) BOROUGH
Walt.Randolf*	Jn.le Boteler*	Jn.le Butelir*
Rd Neel	Mich.Aside (a Lyde)	Galf.le Fisher
Id.rel.Chauntrel	Will.Gosseling	Jn atte Lynde
Galf le Boteler	Rd atte Stanstrete*	Mich.a Lyde
Walt le Borgeys*	Jn.Clymping	Rd.le Pyk
Rad.atte Stanstrete*	Alic.le Turnour	Will.Gosselyn
Matil.rel.Maresch.	Galf.le Fyssher	Jn.Laurens
Jn Pecoc maior	Rob.le Stupere	Jn.le Baker
Rob.le Cradel	Pet.le Turnour	Will.le Tourneur
Mart.le Peec*	Matill.atte Boure	Pet.le Tourneur*
Rd.le Hert	Laur.le Baker	Jn.le Budel
Nich.atte Rydeforde	Nich.Fabro (smith)	God.le Boghier
Will.le Coupe	Jn.atte Lynde	Matil.atte Boure
Will.Wardhech	Will.Stedman	Lucy atte Brome
Will.le Chalener	Ad.Quillard	Will.le Digher
Rob.Godefray*	Tho.le Bakere	Jn.Godefray*
Tho.Bibon	Will.Bochier	Tho.le Glovar*
Rd.Conky	Tho.le Glover*	Walt.Randekyn*
Ad.Cotsyn	Oliver Skilling*	Rd.atte Stanstret*
Pet.atte Linde	Will.Turnour	Oliver Skylling*
Sim.atte Moure	Alic.atte Brome	Laurens le Baker
Rd.le Tournur	Will.le Chalner	Rob.le Stupere
Rd.le Wuchere	Jn.Cole	Nich.Fabro
Rand.de Horsham*	Will.le Dygher	Jn.Marchaunt*
Jn.atte Lynde	Mat.Godelove	Jn.Nel*
Morgan Hugon	Jn.Marchaunt	Ad.Quillard
Will.le Rideler	Rd.le Pek	
Will.le Saltere	Rog.Randolf	
Rob.atte Welle	Jn.Godefrai	
Rob.de Horleye	God.Quillard	
Rob.le Mareschal	Rd.Whychere	
Will.Godeman	Jn.le Bonwyck	
Gilb.atte Boure	Rd.le Burgeis	
Ben.Bockhorn	Nich.Swenge	
Ph.Craddoc	Rog.le Singar	
Will.Elrich		
Galf.Handhamer		
Jn.Moys		
Jn.Pecoc min.		
Will.le Skinnere		
Jn.le Skinnere		
Will.Waryn		

From the end of the 13th century, events continued to underline the importance of Horsham, not just to the local economy but in a wider context, making it a desirable place to settle, build, expand and consolidate. In 1306 the assizes were held in the town for the first time, and from then on Horsham took its turn with Lewes and Chichester. To get some idea of the impact of such an event, the assizes that year dealt with 36 civil and 22 criminal cases, and 21 pleas of complaint, mostly concerning trespass and assault. Imagine how many days it must have taken to get through all that business, and the number of people involved – justices, their retinues and officials, the accused, their witnesses and accusers, witnesses for the prosecution and various juries drawn from local communities – not to mention any 'hangers-on'. These people probably doubled the population of the borough and would have required food and lodging for the duration.

In 1308 a public inquiry into the affairs of the Templar preceptory at Shipley was held in Horsham by royal commissioners, who summoned local men to make up the required juries. This was the conclusion of a campaign against the order, orchestrated from France, which alleged corruption and blasphemy, and resulted in its destruction. County coroners also began to hold courts in Horsham about this time, to conduct the investigations and procedures connected with the discovery of dead bodies, and property owned by wealthy individuals who had died. Two coroners were fined for failing to turn up in Horsham in 1321.

Among the representatives Horsham continued to send to parliaments – held not only in Westminster but also at York, Salisbury, Gloucester and Winchester – were men called le Gretesmyth, le Flechiere, Cok, le Barbour, Nywebakere, Spicer and Jewdry. The national taxation returns contain many other names indicating occupations, such as glover, merchant, wool-beater, and flagon-maker as well as butcher, baker and dyer. These list only taxpayers, and about 30% of the population were exempt as having less than 10s worth of assets. Horsham's wealth and prosperity depended on the success of her traders, their contacts and influences. Even thieves recognised this, like the three who were indicted at Guildford assizes in 1315, for *robbing certain foreign merchants outside Horsham to the west* of goods to the value of £40.

Naming and Spelling

The formation of **surnames** that were inherited may have had something to do with the increase in written records in the 12th and 13th centuries. Until then most people were known by their personal name and some distinguishing by-name, which could refer to where they lived, where they came from, what they did or the office they held, to whom they were related and sometimes to a physical or personal characteristic (a nickname). These by-names were not inherited and one person could be known several different ways during his lifetime. As ownership or regulated tenancies of property became more widespread, so did the need to settle disputes and ensure continuity, and so by-names became fixed and hereditary. Most people in England had a surname by the 15th century. **Spelling**, too, was variable – there were no dictionaries – and only gradually became standardised from the phonetic as printed literature increased during the 17th and 18th centuries.

One of the earliest maps of Britain is called the Gough map and dates from 1350. It includes many, if not most of the places that stood on main routes, and shows a national network of roads radiating from the capital. Among the number of short-distance routes from London to the Channel ports is that running via Dorking and Horsham to Shoreham, so the town was already on a 'recommended route' for travellers. In 1350 the City of London Corporation wrote to Horsham about a complaint they had received that the borough bailiffs had taken matters into their own hands to try to prevent livestock traders by-passing the town, presumably for higher prices. They had arrested some Farnham men who bought such cattle and wrested a promise from them that they would do so no more!

During the first 150 years or so of parliamentary representation, the local MPs do seem to have been genuinely resident, drawn from the traders and craftsmen upon whom the town's prosperity had been built and thoroughly involved in all that was going on locally. We have already seen that not all

Postcard of Horsham Market,
outside the Green Dragon, Bishopric; c.1911.

Horsham market, Bishopric; looking out of town towards the Green Dragon (on the right in the distance).

were upright members of society untouched by scandal. Walter Randekyn first appears on the taxation roll of 1332 as a burgess, and about a year later he was accused of acquiring £20 worth of wine illegally, being involved with wreckers at Worthing, and trespassing, poaching and assaulting servants all on the lands of John de Mowbray. When his wife Alice died in 1351 he undertook to give 6s 8d to the poor of Horsham for 20 years – perhaps as conscience money. He represented Horsham seven times from 1337 and was succeeded by his son (another Walter) who also went to parliaments seven times. Walter the father was murdered in 1357, but although his servant, Joan atte Naldrette, was indicted for being a party to and aiding the felony, she was granted a royal pardon – apparently because she was able to prove her innocence. Walter the son was also a county coroner in 1390, but he was no better than his father, for he was called to account along with John Bradbrugge, the younger, bailiff of Bramber rape, for conspiracy to defraud over legal fines, whereby each received a cut.

In 1421 Horsham was represented by Roger Elyot, chapman (seller of small wares), who was indicted for two hanging offences some six years apart. In 1429 he was accused of breaking into John Dawtre's house in Horsham, assaulting his wife Pernell, and taking a 'maser' or cup worth 6s 8d, a silver girdle worth 20s and three gowns worth 40s. Furthermore, in 1435 he broke into the Southwark home of Sir Hugh Halsham (of West Grinstead) smashed open a chest with an iron bar and stolen two fur-trimmed garments worth 10 marks (a mark was equivalent to 13s 4d). During the trial it appeared that one of the jurors, Stephen Sloughterforth of Warnham, was himself under suspicion, and as Roger too received a royal pardon, it seems that there was more to this case than meets the eye. There were many processes of medieval justice that we would find unfamiliar and puzzling.

Even the more humble of Horsham residents presented temptations to the average thief. Henry Reperose, who had a 'close and buildings' in 1456, had two yards of blanket, a doublet and a yard of kersey to the value of 4s stolen from him by Thomas Cornwall, a carpenter from Lewes.

Green Dragon, Bishopric, c.1920.

Oil painting of the Bishopric, Horsham by J M Gregory (1884).
The Green Dragon is one of the buildings to the right.

By 1500, Horsham not only had its annual fair and twice-weekly market, and played host to both coroners' courts and assizes, but in 1449 the Archbishop of Canterbury had been granted a charter for a weekly market and two annual fairs to be held on his outlier of Marlpost, which included the area now called the Bishopric.[1] Presumably this was capitalising on Horsham's prosperity, and it is possible that what was the Green Dragon public house (now the Olive Branch) where manorial courts were held in the 18th century, was even then a centre of administration, probably the house for the Marlpost beadle.

1   Marlpost lay west of the town, and included land extending from Southwater to Rusper; it had belonged to the archbishopric from before 1086.

Etched print entitled 'Two Bricklayers' from a series depicting trades and professions by Jan Georg van Vliet, also likely to have been the original artist; c.1630.

Chapter Two
Houses in Medieval Horsham (and beyond)

How to approach the study of buildings in a town? The first answer must be 'by looking closely at the structures themselves, and trying to understand what they can tell us' – then to become familiar with the other principal sources such as historic documents, deeds and maps.

The documentary evidence for houses in Horsham before 1300 is scarce, almost all being described as no more than *'tenement'* or *'messuage'* in the *'feet of fines'* – a kind of central registry of property deals. About a dozen of these between 1236 and 1300 have been printed.[2] A few buildings are mentioned briefly in the Chartulary of Sele Priory, near Beeding, over a similar period, and the vicar's 'manse' is noted in 1231.

There is just one house (considerably altered) within Horsham parish but beyond the town, which has been placed firmly within this early period using the technique of dendro-chronology. If suitable samples can be taken, this technique can be very precise about the *'felling date'* of the timber, which we know was generally used within two years of being cut down. In the 1970s, Chennelsbrook, on the Rusper road, was recognised as an 'early example' on stylistic evidence alone. Sincev then a unique (but largely hidden) original window with trefoil heading has been found, and we now know that it was built with timber cut down in the winter of 1295/6.

The first 500 years or so of Horsham's history had laid the foundations for the following centuries, and illustrate how it was that its function as a centre for marketing and administration was established. As a footnote, many people I have met since I arrived in Horsham in 1970 have bemoaned the way the town has been 'spoiled' in that time. As far as buildings are concerned, I tell them first to go round looking at the number of 19th century dates on buildings (over 30) and then study old photographs to see how previous generations treated buildings we would now 'preserve'. Although several important buildings went in the 1950s and '60s, one being removed to the museum at Singleton, we have only lost one complete building since 1970 (Bournes) another has been re-instated (Stan's Way) and a visitor from the past would still be able to find his way around the town centre, even if his eyes were starting out of his head!

Photographs of Chennelsbrook front and rear wing.

2   Sussex Record Society vols 2, 7, 23. Three copies were made of such deals; one for each of the participants and the third, at the 'foot', went to the central 'registry'.

Print of a landscape drawing of
St. Leonard's Forest, 1820.

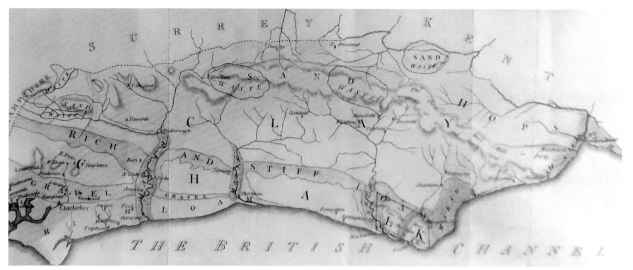

Print of a sketch in map form of the soils of Sussex; date unknown.

It probably survived because it was initially an aisled 'hall' of considerable status and was in a rural setting until relatively recently. It was almost certainly built by one of the de Coombes family from near Steyning, who were among the followers of the de Braose tenants-in-chief. It is only yards away from a motte-and-bailey site that was abandoned in the mid-1100s, and other clues suggest it was a 'leisure facility', as a lodge for hunting. It is one of only four such houses that have been identified so far in West Sussex, three of which have now been dendro-dated to between 1230 and 1300.

The earliest written description in any detail of a dwelling near Horsham comes from the records of Sele Priory, at Beeding, and refers to a property in the Forest of St Leonard in 1285:

> . . . *all the buildings of that tenement well thatched and protected and well enclosed with wooden walls for the most part and with earthen walls round . . .*

A fictionalised, but informed, impression of a house in its early Sussex setting appears in Alfred Duggan's Knight with Armour, imagined in the year 1096:

> *Conversation was impossible on the ride, as the horses struggled in single file, girth-deep in the muddy clay track, through the deep tangled woods of the Weald; but in the evening they crossed the river and rode up the hill to the timber-and-wattle hall that looked northwards to the endless woods of Kent.*

Today we are most familiar with the idea of building from some kind of solid blocks and mortar, relying on the force of gravity to hold the whole thing together. Early houses in Horsham, as elsewhere, were built from the materials that came easily to hand – and here this meant timber, straw, sticks, animal hair, mud, and later on, split sandstone. This is what is meant by the term 'vernacular architecture' – dwellings built by local people from easily-available local materials. Houses like the forest tenement needed frequent renewal, and none have survived except as soil traces found in archaeological excavations, like those at Broadbridge Heath, discovered in advance of the development at Wickhurst Green.

Timber-framed buildings – largely pre-fabricated as open wooden frames, sometimes at a distance from the actual site, sometimes beside an on-site saw-pit dug for the purpose – relied on oak-pegged joints to keep them together, and their flexibility helped them to survive harsh weather or ground settlement. Once jointed together, a giant hand could have picked one up, turned it around and put it down again, without any great disturbance to its basic structure. It was accepted that the wattle-and-daub that filled the spaces and which worked with the flexibility of the framing would need patching or replacement from time to time.

House reconstructed from archaeological evidence at Weald and Downland Museum, Singleton.

'Once jointed together, a giant hand could have picked one up, turned it around and put it down again, without any great disturbance to its basic structure'. (Chilsfold farm, Northchapel).

The earliest houses would have been one-room constructions, open to the rafters, with a central fire on a stone hearth, and the occupants had to be good at slow-burning dry wood, and possibly charcoal, to get the maximum heat for the longest time with the minimum smoke. We must be careful not to imagine that all early buildings were small and wretched. In the 1281 court rolls for Halesowen, Worcestershire, the specifications of a house are given. It was to be the 'dower' house for a woman whose son who was taking over her land on her retirement, and was to be 14 feet wide and 30 feet long between the end walls, with corner posts, three new doors and two windows – an early 'granny annexe'. The main house on the holding must have been at least the same size.

In order to gain some privacy in early open-hall houses, the roof sometimes extended down beyond the eaves to form aisles, and hangings between the aisle-posts then created some kind of screened-off area. A number of different words were used for houses in early records, suggesting there were various kinds of traditional houses that were different in both plan and size. However, while life was still comparatively harsh and basic, governed by sunrise and sunset and revolving around the seasons and demands of land and animals, this open, communal pattern of life continued.

As communities grew and became more organised, and a social structure emerged that was more complex than just peasant and lord, the demand for privacy grew among lesser men, who wanted houses that could fulfil a wide range of more sophisticated functions, and which had a greater degree of comfort and convenience. Screens were inserted to separate 'service' and storage areas from the main living space, and first floors put in at the ends of houses to capitalise on space and provide private units for the master of the house and his family. Existing houses were adapted to meet these needs while new builds incorporated 'modern' features.

Over the hundred years after 1300, about 40 local properties feature in the printed feet of fines and other documents, and examples include shops and a mill:

In 1305:

Nicholas atte Redforde and his wife settled a house and six acres on their daughter Matilda, who had married a Richard Morgan [indicating Welsh origin when names were still descriptive]. Hugh Morgan paid tax as a burgess in 1296, and in the same year the atte Redfordes also settled a house on their son John.

In 1318:

a house and 30 acres went to William, son of William de Assheleye, for £20; in 1330 and 1334 houses went for 100 shillings.

In 1345:

a house and 3 roods cost £10, and in the following year Peter and Isabella le Tournor rented a house and 3 acres for 9 shillings and a rose at Midsummer. [A rose at Midsummer features in several records, probably as a sign of good faith.]

In 1362 the record of a grant made illustrates how much information can be gleaned from one of these early documents:

by Sir Adam Tybay, vicar's chaplain, to John & Agnes Coupere between

W	*formerly Richard atte Stanstret & Oliver Skyllyng*
N	*curtilage of Adam Stykeman, chaplain*
E	*Jn Styks jr*
S	*highway from market place > St Leonard's Forest*

[north side East Street]
+2 tenements also of said John between

W	*William the Smith*
N	*garden of John Randolph*
E	*formerly William the Tanner*
S	*highway from market place > Guildford*

[north side West Street]
Witnesses: John atte Denne, John Randolph, Richard Salter, Robert le Frenshe, Walter Randekyn, Roger Spycer, Robert le Coupere, John Aysmythe, William Glover

Three properties were involved, and the transaction was between 'Sir Adam Tybay, vicar's chaplain' and John and Agnes Coupere. Because the abutments (details of adjoining buildings or features) are given, we can place the first property on the north side of the present East Street, the second two properties on the north side of West Street - that is, part of the development of the burgage sites that flanked the streets. The impression given is very much of a built-up urban scene.

Of the two priests named, Tybay appears to have been one of the three assistants to the vicar (who were stipulated in a document of 1231) and Stykeman was either attached to the chantry 'in the porch', or associated with another of the ecclesiastical bodies with local interests – for example the Archbishop of Canterbury or the Abbey of Fescamp. The personal names show that in most cases people were still being described by what they did, or where they lived, and the range of trades is also urban in character.

In 1367, John Borle let:

2 houses, 2 shops and their land for 2s 6 3/4d to John and Emma Hadresham, and Thomas and Alice Chamberleyn.

In 1369, in a deal between Roger Bushop and Thomas Jewary, the property is described thus:

'Shop with an upper storey (or loft) built thereon, in Horsham, which the said Roger once granted for the life of the said Thomas, abutting South on a tenement of the said Thomas beside Horsham market place, West on a shop of John Basch'.

It is clear that there were permanent retail premises in Horsham by the early 14th century, and by the latter part of the century it is likely that some of these were encroachments onto the original open market-place – weekly 'standings' turned into permanent shops. The evidence of early buildings within and around the Carfax[3] suggest that these developed out of market stalls that began to remain from one market to the next, and then became more and more substantial. The narrow alleys or 'twittens', that re-building has preserved and in some cases imitated, are one feature of modern Horsham that medieval residents would find familiar.

---

3   This name for the centre does not appear until the end of the 1700s, possibly aping Oxford and Exeter, which actually were crossroads. Horsham's unique town centre name is 'The Skarfolkes' (see 1524/5 later).

Passageway from Market Square to Middle Street, Horsham by Sendall's Butcher (rear), 1910.

Pen and ink drawing of the Town Hall, Market Square and the 'Bear'; c.1920.

Pen and ink drawing of Horsham town hall in Market Square from the Causeway side drawn by G Mann, as it was c.1750 with open arches; c.1912.

Horsham – 'Pump Alley' by Glyn Martin, Cambrooke Fine Art Publishers Ltd.

Pump Alley, c.1930.

The ways into Pirie's Place, Talbot or Pump Alley, Colletts Alley, the lanes each side of the stores on the south side of Middle Street, were all laid down early in the town's history, and this is supported by careful examination of the buildings in their vicinity. There were probably others of which only vestiges remain, on the north side of Middle Street and the east side of the Carfax, and the Swan Walk complex is just a modern interpretation of a similar theme.

Artist's impression of Pump Alley; painting thought to be c.1870.

Pump Alley, c.1900.

Oil painting by Edward Bainbridge Copnall (1927) of the farmer's cattle market at Horsham Railway Station.

In some cases these lanes gave access to the 'backsides' of properties, as residents remained in touch with their agricultural roots, tending fruit trees, growing vegetables and hops, keeping livestock such as pigs, goats and poultry. As the market-place was gradually colonised by more permanent buildings, other passages are a reminder of the divisions between different stalls and 'speciality' areas – livestock and butchery, small wares and pedlary, drapery and entertainment. As Middle Street was known as 'Butchers' Row' as late as the 18th century it was almost certainly a 'zoned' butchers' shambles, and three narrow alleys remain to remind us of the passages between blocks of stalls.

Middle Street, 2016.
Courtesy of Rooney & Co estate agents.

Identical views down London Road/Medwin Walk showing 3 and possibly 4 early houses to the left, including Bournes.

East Street in 1910.

West Street in 1910.

Sad demise of Bournes showing the crown-posts – hopefully the last such demolition.

In two cases these 'alleys' were more substantial and are the remains of the link between older north/south 'main roads' through Horsham (Park Street/Denne Road or Back Lane/Friday Street as it was once called, and Springfield/Worthing Road) and the new market-place. East and West Streets surely developed from 'twittens' that served the earliest markets, pre-dating the burgage plots that extend along each side, both north and south.

Like any town, there would have been constant re-building and expanding, but medieval demolitions did not involve a bonfire.

'Probably gaoler's cottage, Horsham' by Thomas Mann; 1830-1845.

Anyone who has spent time looking over medieval buildings will quickly realise that in a 'handmade' world timbers were never wasted but re-used wherever possible. Empty mortices and peg-holes in apparently unnecessary places are calculated to add to the problems and fascination of interpreting early houses.[4] In 1357, in the court rolls of the manor of Wiston, near Steyning, there is a detailed record of what happened to one house in Horsham, when it became surplus to requirements, perhaps as a result of the Black Death which rampaged through England between 1347 and 1350. The house was bought for 66s 9d, the stone roof was dismantled and carted down to Steyning at the cost of 6s 10d, for a repair job, and the timbers sold off in Horsham for 16s 8d. This was a time when the average weekly wage for a building labourer was roughly 2s.

The influence of some families over several generations can be traced through records, and is reflected in a variety of written records. There were the Butlers, the earliest owners of the burgage plots of that name stretching north from the west corner of North Walk, adjacent to and part of the site of one of the earliest Horsham gaols.

In spite of the efforts of previous owners, this building still contains the framework of the gaoler's house.
Courtesy of Rooney & Co estate agents.

---

4   The term *'ships' timbers'* has found a far more sensible interpretation; it applied to the *quality* of the timber, just as today we speak of *'marine ply'*

In 1307, Galfrid le Boteler was among the witnesses to the endowment of the Holy Trinity chantry, by the north door of the parish church, and on the evidence of the 1296 tax list was well-to-do. John Butiler comes high on the next two lists, in 1327 and 1332 and the family represented Horsham at parliaments over 58 years. Richard Wakehurst (the county member) and others established a chantry in 1447 in memory of Henry Botiler and his wife.

In 1423 Henry Frenssh left a missal, chalice and vestments to the Holy Trinity chantry, as well as 20d for the parish clerk, possibly then living in part of the house now called Minstrels. Robert le Frainceys was town bailiff in 1288, Frensshes were MPs 12 times during the 14th century (1300s) and the borough survey of 1611 mentions *a tenement called the Red Lion, formerly Frensshes'* on the corner of West Street and Carfax where Waterstones bookshop now stands.

Formerly The Red Lion – now Waterstones, 2016.
Courtesy of Rooney & Co estate agents.

In a probate inventory of 1612, the Red Lion (then owned by the Tredcroft family) is described as having a hall, chamber, parlour and little parlour on the ground floor, a little chamber 'at the stayers head' four chambers on the first floor including 'Old Bottings chamber', and three garrets, apart from the usual offices – kitchen, buttery, bakehouse, brewhouse, all with lofts – and cellars. Either the earliest building had been considerably expanded over the decades, or (more likely) it was an early 16th century (1500s) re-build, remnants of which could be seen when the bookshop was refurbished. The Tredcrofts moved to Horsham from Billingshurst in the 16th century, and in 1564, Thomas 'a tailor, of Horsham' died. Robert the innkeeper, who died in 1611 was his son, and a grandson, another Robert, was a vintner who supplied wine for the church communions.

The Red Lion in 1898 (Duke's). This was fully-floored, close-studded and jettied around the corner.

RED LION INVENTORY 1611

The true inventory. . . of household stuffe of Robert Tredcrafte of Horsham . . . deceased . . . 1611 . . . taken and praised by Richard White, Edward Parkhurst, Thomas May and Thomas Sharpe (WSEO Ep1/29/106/2)

In the [upper] chamber
Imprimis one standing bedstedle with green Curtens two lowe bedstedles II ... 1 flocked i quilt ii Rugges iii blankets iii coverlets iiii fetherboulsters ii father pillows iii payer of sheet & ii pillow
Itm of his wearing apparel iii . . . iiii jerkins iii payer of breeches ii closes i gone iii sheets v [bands] ii hats [v] payer of stockings & ii woollen . . .
Itm one trunk with xii payer of [pil]low cotes therein
Itm one joyned chest with x . . . tablecloths whereof ii be diaper & xxvi towels therein
Itm one other joyned chest with ii . . . shorts therein
Itm one presse one looking glass one little desk & a liney wolsey Colvercloth
Itm ii bibles one old pultons abridge . . . two books of Comon prayer
Itm one dozen of silver spoones one alle silver salt one litle salt viii silver bowles and one beaker all wayinge allmost vi poundes
Itm one chest with his evidences there . . . sed stoole iii little chests one peece of new wollen cloth and one peece ofnewe cawse cloth for napkins
Itm one sack with £viii of lambes woll therein
Itm two tapestrie coverletts
Itm three brushes i urynall & certen glasse bottles
Itm of ready money n his purse

In the Parlor
Itm ii tables with frames i lyvery cubbeed ii formes i chayer ii carpetts one Cubberd cloth x cushions i payer of brandyrons and certen paynted clothes

In the hall
Itm ii tables i forme viii joyned stools iii chayers i cubberd one litle round table vii cushions i old carpet ii cubed clothes i payer of brandirons i flyer panne i payer of tonges iii pot hangers one piece of iron & certen paynted clothes

In the litle Parlor
Itm ii tables i stool i cushion & one payer of playing tables

In the chamber over the parlor
Itm ii standing bedstedles ii truckebedstedles ii fether beddes iii fether bolsters iiii pillows ii flockbeddes iii flockboulsters iiii blanketts iiii coverings & i payer of curtens
Itm one table with a frame i carpet i joyned forme i other forme iiii joyned stooles i chayer & i cushion

In the chamber at the stayers hedd
Itm one truckle bedstedle one featherbed i blanket one bolster one pillow one presse i chest one hamper and shelves

In the middle chamber
Itm ii bedstedles i fetherbedd i fether boulster i pillow ii flockbeddes ii boulsters [ii] coveringes & one blankett

In the Parlor chamber
Itm two bedstedles one per of curtens ii fetherbeds three fether boulsters one flock boulster two coverings two blankets & fowre pillows
Itm one table and frame five stooles one jorned forme one other forme two chayers one cushion & one carpett

In the chamber over the hall
Itm i standing bedstedle one fetherbedd ii fetherboulsters two pillowes one Rugge ii mattres i blanket and curtens Itm one cubbere i lyvery table i longe table with a frame two joyned formes one liverie cubberd viii cushions ix stools one carpett one chayer one payer of brandirons one payer

of bellowes one empty chest one payer of playing tables & one white cubberd cloth
Itm one chest xi payer of sheetes therein two boxes & one litle chest with five dozen of Fine napkins and one od one five dozen & three odd napkins of flame & hemp with painted clothes about the room and curtness for the windows

In old Bottinges chamber
Itm one bedstedle with curtness one fetherbed and bolster two pillows one blanket one covering one truckle bedstedle with a fether bedd and boulster two pillowes one blankett and a covering
Itm one wicker chayer one other chair four Cushions one trunk with xliii sheets therein and one stole

In the folkes chamber
Itm twoe bestedles one flockbed and boulster one coveringe one blanket & one payer of sheets

In the middle Garrett
Itm twoe bedstedles & a lynnen tester

In the Further Garrett
Itm twoe bedstedles one bagge of hoppes divers varyers Crocks potts & bottles one side sadle one rodd sadle xxx lb of hempen tyre xii lb two six trugges iii lb of wool and other basketts and lumberment

In the buttrie chamber
Itm twoe bedstedles with curtness one downe bed & boulster twoe downe pillowes one fetherbed and boulster twoe pillowes twoe Rugges twoe blanketts twoe mattres twoe payer of sheets and twoe pillowbeeres
Itm one table wth a frame fower ioyned formes twoe chayers three stooles one liverie Cubberd one Carpett one Cubberdcloth twoe Cushions one payer of playing tables one payer of brandirons one payer of tonges the paynted clothes about the chamber and curtens for three Windowes

In the Backhowse loft
Itm twoe bedstedles twoe fether bedde fower fether Boulsters twoe coveringes twoe blankets one close stoole one table and one forme one stoole and one skreene

In the kitchinge loft
Itm one bedstedle and Curtness one father bedd two bolsters two pillows one Rugge one blanket one truckle bedstedle and one flockbed
Itm one table with a frame three formes two stools one chair one Cushion and the paynted clothes about the Roome

In the Brewehowse loft
Itm three payer of Canvas sheets
Itm twoe Coopes a heape of Chacks a trest a still a brake ii payer of boots ten Couple of Codd fish & other lumbermen

In the litle loft next
Two hoggesheddes with salt one hogs head with vinegar two baskets and one flaskett

In the Brewhowse
Itm one fornace and brewing vessels a sack of wood a heap of pales certen Caskes twoe loads of Coles a wollen wheele and other lumberment

In the milkehowse
Itm one kneadinge trowe one boultinge hutch i tubbe i Crock of butter i powdringe tubbe i tubbe with pease a half bushel i tubbe with tallow i hymnal i hanging Cubberd i Charne & shelves and lumbermen Itm one Tubbe with meale viii fletches of bacon and one breast of beefe

In the kitchen
Itm fowre iron pottes two brasse potts iiii dripping pannes one brasse Caldron ii brasse ketles one warming panne vii brasse posnetts & iiii Chaffing dishes
Itm viii spittes twoe fryinge pannes twoe gridyrons one iron morter one stone morter one bushell measure ii racks one payer of

brandirons iii pot hangers one iron peele ii fier pannes and one iron to put before frying pannes
Itm one latin ladle one skimmer one slice ii brasse spoones one skonce iii payer of pothoocks one fleshhoock one Clever one Course one shredding knife one chopping knife one breddgrate one beame & vii lb weights and one mustard ball Itm xii woodden dishes iii woodden platters iii potlides iiii ladles vi dozen trenchers iiii bucketts one cubberd one moulding table ii dressers one from iiii shelves and one chayer Itm of pewter two square plates vi round plates iii basons iii ewers iii chargers iii dozen of pewter dishes v small basens iii Culloners xvii platters xxvi round pottengers ix squared pottengers iiii Candlesticks iii round cupps one egg plate xxii spoones all wayinge xxxiii nayle and iiii lb at viiid the pounde

In the Buttrye
Itm of pewter xii platters x . . . dishes v basons one . . . dish . . . chamber potts two wyne p. . . pottes xxi quart pots xvii pynt pots iii half pinte potes ii quarter pinte pottes two . . . ells & two saltes all wayinge xxiii nayle at viiid the pounde Itm viii laten Candlesticks
Itm xii stone potter
Itm one Great Cubberd one litle Cubberd one bread byn vii Shelves one little old Chest three dozen of playing Cardes one . . . tankard one flask & one lanthorne
Itm vi veny glasses vi napkins ii tableclothes and . . .

In the Beere Sellar
Itm v Brlle whereof two full of beere

In the Wine Sellar
Itm one hogshedd of claret wyne half a hogshedd of white wine one R[un]dl[et] of . . .one Rundlet of Wine ka. . .ell. . . vinegar xi . . .hogs[hedd] & vii emty runlets
Itm one pewter flagon one buckinge tubbe one C . . . arrers and a press

In the Gates
Itm xl cordes of wood
Itm Itm twoe sowes and twoe shootes
Itm iiii tw. . .a. . .bridle. . .pe and chaines
Itm Twoe kyne and two Calves
Itm three hogtrowes ix pieces of timber and one ladder
Itm . . . hennes one Cock three ducks and one mallard

In the Stable
Itm one half peck one gallon one curry combe & one mane combe
Itm inch boorde and plankes over the stable

In the Ostrie
Itm twoe dozen bottles of hay four hundred of course momtens and panel boorde one tubbe and four bushels of otes

In the Barne
Itm the Haie by estimation iiii lodes
Itm twoe ladders twoe prongs one shovel and one wheelbarrowe

In the feilds abroad
Itm one mare and a Colt
Itm one nag seised for herriot

In the Garner
Itm twoe quarters of malt three quarters of otes fower bushels of Rye and one shovel

In the slayinge howse
Itm twoe hundred of pales

In the Barne hired of Mr Nye
Itm eight lodes of Hay
Itm . . . lode of straw
Itm . . . ast a lode of Raile posts

In Buckley Wood
Itm in tymber hewed sawed and standinge and also in wood

In the Garden
Itm wett clothes viz twoe payer of hempen sheetes one payer of holland sheets three Canvas sheets one table cloth viii napkins and one towell

(This is followed by items in nine rooms at 'The howse called the Ancker' which was leased to Thomas May who died three years later).

The Botting family, in turn, can be linked with the house on the burgage plot opposite the Black Jug[5] in North Street, known in the late 16th century as 'The George, formerly Bottings', and they included a shoemaker and two butchers at that time. In 1430, the junction of Denne Road and East Street was called Stanestreet cross, and Richard atte Stanestret is mentioned in early documents as a wealthy burgess, property owner and MP over 21 years. On the corner of Denne Road is one of Horsham's most impressive early houses, now divided between a newsagent and a restaurant, which was known variously as Bishop's and Grace's from the 17th century. It is characteristic of a group of high status local buildings, whose central open hall was flanked by one or two cross-wings.

The George, formerly Bottings, after renovations in the 1970s. The northern wing was renovated in 1984.

The Hurst Arms in North Street, 1989; now The Black Jug.

5   The original Black Jug (or Jack) was in the adjoining building, now the China Brasserie

The next documentary marker for Horsham is the taxation list of 1524/5 when property owners and/or residents were listed by street – East, West, North, South and Skarfolkes. East Street then corresponded with the line of Park Street/Denne Road, South Street was The Causeway, and Skarfolkes just part of the current Carfax (west and north). A list of those in 'Marlpost', which included the Bishopric and Worthing Road, is given at the same time.

Please note that the following tables are listed in pounds, shillings and pence.

THE BOROUGH OF HORSHAM

Taxation in £sd generally based on value of goods, unless otherwise indicated i.e. L = lands, F = fees, A = yearly wages, D yearly wages of day labourers, x = no basis given; £1 & £1.6.8 usually on wages

THE ESTE STRETE
1524

John Dungate		2		
Robert Ryxhardson		5		
Edward Terell		3		
Rychard Ive		13	6	8
Rychard Sowten		6	13	4
John Wykyn		L5		
John Bokar		2	13	4
Robert Bokar		26	13	4
Henry Fylpott		2		
George Repkyn		L	3	
John Gamyll, pynner		3		
John Swan hys servant	A	1		

Rychard Ryvhow hys servant	A	1		
Andrew Robynson		4		
Rychard Froyle		6		
John Dykynson	D	1		
Rychard a Wode	D	1		
Nicholas Smalpece	D	1		
Bartylmew Thurstyll	D	1		
Henry Owton	D	1		
John Gyllet Frenssheman	D	1		
Rychard Warde	D	1		
Rychard Jakett	D	1		
Thomas Roser	D	1		

1525

Hamlett Pynnar	D	1	
John Froyle	D	1	
John Owten	D	1	

THE WESTRETE
1524

Jamys Monyer		3	6	8
Nycholas Hurst		40		
John Saltos hys servant	A	2		
Roger Oswy		2		
Rychard Ive junior		2		
Thomas Cok		2		
Wyllyam Page		2		
John Jenyn		2		
Henry Baker	x	1	6	8
Thomas Aylesbury	D	1		
Anne Dalton	D	1		
Wyllyam Hinde	x	1	6	8
Rychard Starr	x	1	6	8
John Sowter	x	1		
Thomas Mylward	x	1		
John Weller shomaker	x	1		
Thomas Amys	x	1		
Rychard Burndysch	x	1		

1525

William Hynde		1	
Richard Starr		1	
John Goldyng	D	1	
Thomas Aylesbury	D	1	
Anne Dalton	D	1	

THE NORTHSTRETE
1524

Emery Tusman		6	13	4
John Aly[n]son		6	13	4
Henry Bull		2		
Rychard Bone		2		
Thomas Wuller		2		
Margery Wodsyll		20		
John Bottyng		2		
Thomas Barnefeld		2		
John Bedyll		26	13	4
Wyllyam Prest hys servant	A	2		
John Rychardson	A	1		
Robert Carpenter	A	1		
Rychard Alyngham	A	1		
Rychard Robert	A	1		
Thomas Clarke	A	1		
Henry Tully	D	1		
Edward Bassett	D	1		

1525

William Prest	G	2
John Rychardson	D	1
Richard Alyngham	D	1

THE SOUTHSTRETE
1524

Avery Bartwyke Esquier	L	F	54	6	8

and ys decayed sins the lone by the reason that he hath graunted the office of the controllership
of the porte of Chichester to Thomas Awcokk and also ys decayed further of 4 marks in londes that he hath given to Eleynore hussay his daughter in law

Edmond Says	53	6	8
Elyzabeth Foys	53	6	8

and ys decayed £11 sins the lone by the death of Richard Grover of Godylmyng which ys deceased & left nothing to pay his debts and also ys further decayed £5 by the death of one Rafe Furber of Shoreham whys ys deceased & left nothing

Harry Foys	26	13	4
Wyllyam Pudon	10		
John Rose	2		
Wyllyam Danyell	6	13	4
Henry Mychell	20		
Jone Lede (widow)	2		
Wyllyam Onsty	2		
Roger Alen	6		
John Wuller	4		
John Glover hys servant	A	1	
John Newman	3		
John Hadman	2		
John Storer	40		
Rychard Skynnar	2		
The londes of the Fraternity of Seynt John & Seynt Anne in yerely value	L	8	
Rychard Grenyar	x	1	
Edward Alderton	x	1	
Henry Cadman	x	1	
Robert Heywode	x	1	
Robert Gorynge	x	1	6 8
Robert Stroger	x	1	
Raynold Myles	x	1	
Nycholas Grenyar	x	1	
Rychard Brandon	x	1	
John Thomas	x	1	
Thomas Harryson	x	1	
Rychard Mornsale	x	1	
Thomas Mylys	x	1	

1525

John Hurst	L	2
Edward Holond	D	1
Thomas Molyng	D	1
Thomas Saunder	D	1
William Waterman	D	1
Thomas a Dene	D	1
Thomas Wryght	D	1

THE NORTHSTRETE
1524

Emery Tusman	6	13	4
John Aly[n]son	6	13	4
Henry Bull	2		
Rychard Bone	2		

Thomas Wuller	2		
Margery Wodsyll	20		
John Bottyng	2		
Thomas Barnefeld	2		
John Bedyll	26	13	4
Wyllyam Prest hys servant	A	2	
John Rychardson	A	1	
Robert Carpenter	A	1	
Rychard Alyngham	A	1	
Rychard Robert	A	1	
Thomas Clarke	A	1	
Henry Tully	D	1	
Edward Bassett	D	1	

1525

William Prest	G	2
John Rychardson	D	1
Richard Alyngham	D	1

THE SKARFOLKES
1524

Rychard Busshop	30		
John Alyn, mercer	6		
John Capelen	10		
Thomas Elys	16	13	4
Rychard Warde	6	13	4
Rychard Sharpe	20		
John a Godyshalf	6	13	4
Rychard Turner	x	1	
Wyllyam Smalham	x	1	
Rychard Barwyke	x	1	
Thomas Sandsale	x	1	
Wyllyam Gate	x	1	
John Tully	x	1	
Wyllyam Barowe	x	1	
Rychard Roser	x	1	
John Snellyng	x	1	
Thomas Rydrede	x	1	
Olyver Wyllyams	x	1	

1525

John Aylwerde	2	
Henry Snellyng	2	
Thomas Herdyng	2	
John Turner	D	1
John Tely	D	1
Thomas Rode	D	1
Nycholas Sharpe	D	1

MARLEPOSTE
1524

Thomas Trowar	4			
Thomas Holbroke	20			
Walter Skynner	10			
John Pylfold	20			
Rychard Ford	6	13	4	
John Barkar	6	13	4	
Wyllyam [On]sty	L	4	13	4
Thomas Heyleyng	2			
Nicholas Grenyar	6	13	4	
Nele M...a	...			
John Pylfold	20			
Rychard Fust	2			
Wyllyam Pylfold	30			
Harry Pylfold	3			
Thomas Bocher	2			
Thomas Sayars	5			
Symon Fuller	2			
Thomas Jope	5			
Thomas Pylfold	20			
Rychard Stydolf	20			
John Ingram	20			
Wyllyam Pancras	20			
Thomas S.	...			
John Fraunces, Frencheman	...			
John Gatland, servant to John Barker	...			
John Hurrok	D	1		
Robert Dorant	D	1		
John Weller	D	1		
John Davy	D	1		
Rychard Warde	D	1		
John Hatchett	D			
Robert Wattes	D			
Wyllyam Bocher	D	1		
Rychard Master	D	1		
Thomas Sylkden	D			
John Fraunces a Fracheman, servant to Wyllyam Waller (in the arte of tanning)	A	2		

Remains of the high class cross-wing house within the present Nationwide Building Society. Note the high quality moulding of the cap and cushion of the crown-post, the deeply-gouged mould under the curved tie-beam, and the 'fillet' of wood that was between the two side braces to the tie, which are now missing. In the background is the crown-post with down-braces marking the rear wall of the cross-wing.

Watercolour painting of 'Bishops' by Maria Hurst.

Carfax cottages with Horsham slate roofs by Gustav George De Paris; the cottages were sited on the central island where the NatWest bank now stands.

As a general rule only about 70% of the population were liable for tax, the rest being too poor, and even then tax evasion was not unknown! Of the 127 people rated in the borough, and judging purely on modern socio-economic criteria, five were wealthy, 11 middle-class, 39 lower middle-class and 79 employed working class. Among the most comfortable-off were well-established Horsham families like the Foys (Voices), Hursts, Michells and Pilfolds (in Marlpost). Four of the five wealthiest lived in South Street, while the rest were fairly evenly distributed through the town, and many of those taxed on the lower assessments were obviously servants or employees. A tailor, butcher and shoemaker were among the middle-class, two of them living in the Skarfolkes, along with a mercer and weaver. It is not too fanciful to imagine someone like Richard Busshop, taxed on £30, living in the house on Denne Road, and owning another in the middle of the Carfax, where the remains of a high class cross-wing house can be found within the present Nationwide Building Society. Thomas Elys may well have carried on his business in one of the buildings we know existed on both sides of Middle Street, *'formerly Butchers' Row'*; perhaps he traded out of the building that stood on the old site of Glayshers, identified as one or two shops with shuttered counters and now at the Weald and Downland Open Air Museum. Or was it from part of the long range on the west side of Colletts Alley? The evidence of these buildings points to centuries of demolition and re-development.

The house extending south from Pirie's Alley and facing onto the Carfax, now in three occupations, is an almost intact example of a style known as a 'Wealden' and may have housed a man like John Alyn, mercer, almost certainly father of twins Matthew and James, the first of whom was vicar of Horsham by 1574, the latter master of Collyer's Free School in 1567. The building is large enough to have housed both a large family and a business, and was one of several on a burgage plot called The Chequer. On the opposite side of the Carfax was not only a fine house, later known as Bornes,[6] fit to house someone like Richard Sharpe, the tailor, but also a lesser dwelling, part of which appears in an early photograph and was possibly suited to a weaver or fletcher.

---

6   Demolished with the development of Swan Walk

West Street – original site of what is now 'Between the Lines', c.1984.

West Street – original site of where 'Greggs' is today, c.1984.

At this time William Daniel was the parish clerk, and then lived in a house abutting the churchyard (now Flagstones) cheek by jowl with MPs and tax collectors like Avery (or Alfred) Bartwyke – once controller of customs at Chichester – and Edmund Says, as well as Elisabeth and Harry Foys (Voyce), widow and second son of Richard who died in 1513, and who was later remembered with his wife in monumental brasses in the church (only Elisabeth's survives).

Each side of East Street and West Street were burgage plots fronting on the Carfax, that had long been divided up into smaller plots to take advantage of the tracks that linked the market place with St Leonards Forest (east) and Marlpost (west). Several of the under-tenants must have been well-off, judging from the houses that once were there. Along the north side of the present East Street are the remains of (or evidence for) three cross-wing houses, and on the opposite side of a fine wealden attached to a 'terrace' of four or five artisans' premises. A 'pinner', fuller and two glovers once traded, and probably lived, on this side of town, all associated with the clothing trade. John Gamyll, the pinner, was so prosperous that two of his servants were taxpayers. Although Richard Ive lived in the old East Street, he owned a property in West Street that he let out to his son, also Richard, a shoemaker.

John Jenyn lived in West Street, and from other records we know he was either a surgeon or hosier (or both?) and lived in a house called 'Grenehurst' or Greners. This may well have been the three-bay building demolished in the 1960s to make way for the modern tile-hung block – also in three units – that now contains Greggs (2015). Fragmentary evidence for another early building has been identified almost opposite (Between the Lines in 2015) just enough to establish the historic width of the street. We cannot be sure who was then living in the house on the Red Lion site, but Nicholas Hurst, the smith, rated at £40, was living in a house called Haynes, owned by a Michell. He had at least one servant, and when he died in 1534, left three anvils and other tools to his son, Richard, as well as three other houses and land, and yet another *little house called Harpers* to his daughter, Jane. A descendant of his, Robert, was a tailor in 1703 when he bought 'Bolters' (15/16 The Causeway) from the son of a wealthy vicar of Horsham, Nathaniel Tredcroft – another branch of the Billingshurst family.

Northern jetty bracket, now inside first-floor front room. The mortices for close-stud timbering can be seen in the girder, top centre.

As the town became increasingly developed, some of the property records that survive give more precise site descriptions, so that we can make a guess at its position. For example, two deeds (1611 & 1614) on the same property (a messuage, 2 shops and a garden) described it as bounded by the *'king's highway S, W and N'* and by a property *'belonging to the heirs of John Ellis on E'*. Apparently not a burgage, it is most likely that it was one of the 'island' buildings, probably in Butchers' Row. These buildings exploited both frontages, north and south.

By the 18th century the heyday of timber-framed building was passed, although there are one or two fine examples of post-medieval houses built in the last flourish of the tradition by contemporary men of substance.

The front ranges of Bolters (dendro-dated to 1500) and of the Museum, 11 Market Square, and the building on the Red Lion burgage, all would have presented the overhanging jettied fronts and close-timbering that are most familiar to the general public as 'Tudor' or 'Jacobean'.

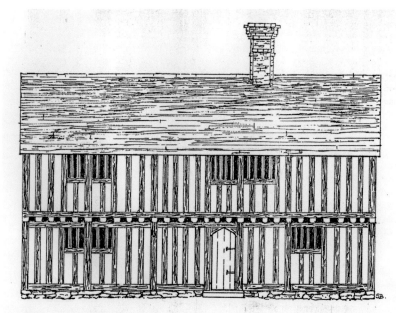

'Bolters' as it appeared circa 1560, by Sylvia Bright

'Horsham' by Glyn Martin,
Cambrooke Fine Art Publishers Ltd.

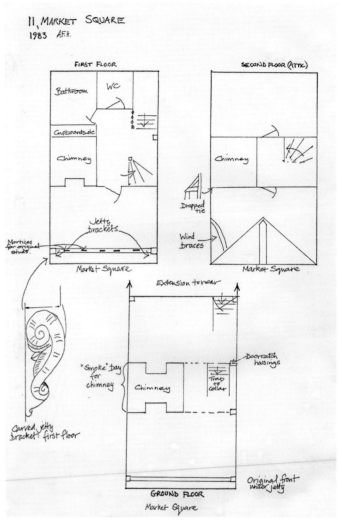

Floor plan of 11 Market Square.

11 Market Square, built before 1611,
once a double-jettied Tudor town house.

Watercolour painting of Park House, Horsham; signed and dated 'H S Syms' and 'April 4 1865'.

15/16 The Causeway, 2016 (Bolters).
Courtesy of Rooney & Co estate agents.

Down East Street (and probably West Street) spaces that had been cultivated land or garden 'closes' were filled in with a rash of buildings, which often recycled old timbers, usually intended to be plastered over or in-filled with brick, and whose timbering was less than impressive as it was not intended to be seen. That townspeople were still prosperous traders is demonstrated in the history of its free school – Collyer's – and in the move to more modern styles of building, anticipated by the replacement of the timber-framed building on the Cockmans burgage site (Park House) in the 1690s, Mr Tredcroft's house of 1703 (the original core of the Manor House) in the Causeway, and Springfield Park, c1758, Samuel Blunt's house on Marlpost.

Mr Tredcroft's (Manor House); Grimm 1789.

Drawing of teazel joint.

Chapter Three
A General Introduction to Timber-framed Construction

During the period 1275 to 1550, most houses in this region were built on **box-frame** principles, from barely seasoned oak. The size of these houses is described by the number of its **bays** – a bay being the distance between two pairs of **principal posts**. Principal posts extend from ground cill to eaves-plates and are held together at the top by a horizontal timber called a **tie**.

Medieval (pre-1530) houses of this type in this area generally have a **crown-post** roof. A crown-post stands upon the middle of each tie that connects a pair of principal posts. A timber running the length of the house in the middle of the roof space – **a purlin** – is supported on these crown-posts. Each pair of rafters is pegged at the apex and connected by a **collar**, which rests across the purlin. The collars are generally **halved** with a **dove-tail** to the rafters, less often tenoned into a mortice.

The assembly of two principal posts, tie and crown-post is called a **truss**. These trusses were either **closed**, having a mid-tie and filled in with wattle and daub, as at each end of the hall, or **open**, without a mid-tie, as over the centre of a two-bay open hall. The crown-post on a closed truss was usually braced down to the tie, and up to the collar-purlin, with the principal posts braced down from the **jowl** to the mid-tie. Principal posts were generally jowled or thicker at the top, in order to accommodate the complicated jointing of **eaves-plate**, **post** and **tie**. This thickening was achieved by using a quartered tree-trunk with the root end at the top, and is sometimes described as a **root-stock**. The profile of these jowls can help towards determining a date range.

Carpenters constructing a timber-framed building, 1531.

'Carpenters' from *The Arts in the Middle Ages and The Period of the Renaissance* by Paul Lacroix (1874).

'Companion Carpenter' from *The Arts in the Middle Ages and The Period of the Renaissance* by Paul Lacroix (1874).

Watercolour, quite possibly by G. Mann.
Carfax, facing The Crown and Collet's Alley.
Note the stone-clad roof.

Hand-coloured aquatint engraving of Penshurst Place, Kent by Joseph Farrington, Royal Academy;
published by J & J Boydell, Shakespeare Press on 1 June 1795; original engraving by J C Stadler.

All the joints of the frame were fastened together with oak pegs. The spaces between the timbers of the frame were originally filled with **wattle**, made from woven sticks or split laths and sprung into place, covered thickly with **daub**, a mixture of clay, animal hair, dung and water. Regular applications of lime-wash were made both inside and out, as a preservative and fire-proofing. If the roof pitch is fairly steep it may have been thatched originally, although this is not an infallible guide. Otherwise the roof would have been covered with tiles or Horsham stone slabs.

As well as considering structure, it is important to remember plan. The medieval house was generally only one room wide, or **single-pile**, although if the house was wide enough, secondary partitions could be introduced. The principal unit consisted of a single room of one or two bays, open from ground to rafters – the **open hall** of the hall house. The only form of heating would have been an open hearth towards the centre of the hall. At either or both ends of the hall there could be **floored bays**, designated as **solar** and **services**. As an alternative to a floored bay, and to achieve more living space, a framed 'box' of two or more bays could be built at right-angles to the open hall, forming a **cross-wing**. These often survive after a hall has been rebuilt or replaced.

The **solar** tended to contain private rooms for the house-owner and his family, sometimes with a first-floor **garderobe** (en-suite 'loo'), and the **services** to be where provisions were kept and food prepared, with additional storage room above. Early kitchens were often contained within structures detached from the main dwelling, which may later be converted into houses.

There were nearly always two opposing doors at one end of the hall, linked by the **cross-passage**, which was sometimes part of the hall, sometimes partially screened, sometimes within a narrow bay of its own, sometimes within the floored end so being **undershot**. This passage almost always abutted the services or '**low**' end of the hall, lying beyond the single open hearth. Where there was a separate solar, it would lie beyond the opposite end of the hall – the '**high**' or '**dais**' end, so called after the raised platform found in the halls of larger houses like Penshurst Place.

Summary of medieval plan types:

3 or more bays with aisles
4 bay 'norm' of 2 bay hall flanked by floored ends
(service & solar)
    High (solar) & low (service) ends usually of 1 bay
    Cross entry or passage at low end of hall, or within
    service
2 bay hall + single floored end (3 bay)
Single bay hall flanked by floored ends (3 bay)
Single bay hall + single floored end (2 bay)
Cross-wing (2-5 bays) in place of either or both
floored ends[7]

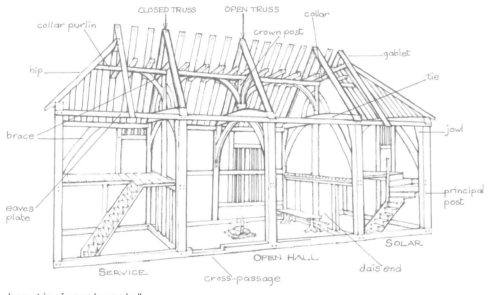

Isometric of open house hall

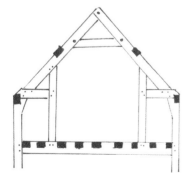

Roof constructed with 'dropped'
or 'interrupted' ties.

Summary of roof types:

Sans-purlin with early features from c1230
(can persist later over humble dwellings)
Crown struts without purlins (movement
towards crown post)
Crown-post and central purlin (the medieval
'norm')
Clasped side-purlin with queen struts and
wind-braces
Side-purlin with raking struts and wind-
braces
Butt-purlins and butt rafters

The desire to control smoke, coupled with changes in social requirements, drove developments in house construction. Sometimes this might involve constructing a two bay hall with one bay floored from start, or a framed **smoke-bay** or **smoke hood** could be introduced into an open hall at first-floor level, pre-dating the eventual **chimney**. Once some kind of smoke control was introduced it was no longer necessary to have an open hall, and these were either floored over in stages, or all at once, to give extra first-floor rooms.

New houses were then planned and built with smoke-bays or chimney stacks, and were fully storied from the start. Changes in roof construction made it possible to use the attic space. Instead of a central **collar purlin**, supported by crown-posts, and collars linking each pair of rafters, a purlin was laid along each side of the roof, supported with struts (and sometimes a collar) at each tie. This did away with the need for a collar for each pair of rafters, and opened up the potential of the roof space for storage, and much more. This was the **through** or **clasped side-purlin** roof, with **queen** struts, or **raking** struts. As time went on, these purlins were morticed (butted) into principal rafters, at first **in-line** or later, **staggered**, to spread the strain of the joints with the rafters. Economies of timber were introduced, such as half-length rafters tenoned into the purlins.

With side-purlin roofs over fully-floored houses and smoke-bays or chimneys and the development of lofts, attics and garrets for both storage and additional living space, the proportions of houses began to change. The **dropped** or **interrupted tie** was introduced c.1580; this construction supported the attic floor on new ties below eaves level and interrupted the internal ties at eaves' level, easing the passageway through, and so increasing both head height and fully accessible roof space.

---

7   These often survive independently, in association with later rebuilding of the
    hall

Generally, the sixteenth century (1500-1600) was a period of **transition**, as old houses were converted to meet rising expectations and new houses built with these changes planned in from scratch. During this transitional period a great many small houses were built, many on former 'waste' ground, at the edges of commons and on the roadsides. At first these were simple constructions with integral smoke-bays; later they would have end stacks, external or internal.

Houses were built that still reflected traditional plans and methods of construction, but incorporated the 'modern' innovations. The 'solar, hall, service' model became the 'parlour, hall, kitchen' with the old 'cross-entry' blocked by a stack that served both hall and kitchen, and developed into a 'baffle' or 'lobby-entry'. Although the central position for a multi-flue stack was favoured, as this provided the maximum benefit to the most number of rooms, external stacks set against the side of the house were a variation, and a display of these could be a status symbol.

Fully floored houses needed only a single stair, and this could rise beside a stack or be housed in an attached 'turret' or 'vyse'. The new styles and plans that were successful, survived and developed into the standard buildings of the seventeenth century and beyond; one move was towards **double-pile** or two rooms wide, which provided extra challenges by way of roof alignments. As time went on, timber-framing became less socially desirable, and those who could afford to, faced up their old buildings to hide the 'old-fashioned' construction, and eventually built from the beginning in brick, stone and flint.

Postcard of North Chapel, North Street Horsham, 1901 – its three chimneys convey social status.

Rough sketch of old chimney just before it was taken down in Butchers Row (Middle Street) Horsham: Nov. 14 1877.

Late functional framing with skimpier timber and smaller panels.

This piece of framing survived in the King's Head car park until the development of Pirie's Place.

Chapter Four
Case Studies

Much as one would like to, it is unreasonable to provide the details of every known historical building in the town, so it becomes a matter of selection, which will never please everyone.

'LOST' BUILDINGS

Glayshers
Bournes
Tudor Cafe
Bishopric terrace
Greenhurst
Fawns
Normandy
Butchers Row
Barkers
Perry Place

West side of the Carfax in 1870. This photograph shows the medieval house 'Barkers' with a Horsham stone slab roof.

Of the thirteen simple open-hall houses that can be identified, one is from early photographs and two others from drawings taken at the time they were demolished, and they have been named as our 'best guess':

*And Henry Patching likewise holds one messuage, a garden with the appurtenances, **late Barkers**, being a portion of a Burgage, by the rent by the year payable (2d)[8]*

Barkers has been named from its position in the 1611 survey, as part of a burgage plot; Robert Barker, a glover, died in 1558.

And that Arthur Woodgate likewise holds one messuage, with barn, backside and garden to the same adjoining, with the appurtenances, late Allens and formerly Holbrooks[9], being one entire Burgage, by the rent payable (1s)

8   Taken from the 1611 written survey, which is printed in both William Albery's books on Horsham
9   Thomas Holbrooke was assessed at £20 tax in 1524 under Marlpost

Reconstruction of Greners.

Greners was built on a part of the burgage that ran along the south side of West Street: The names given for earlier owners of this burgage were of long-standing in Horsham, but the building has been named from a series of sixteenth century records which contain details of 'abutments' – the adjoining properties – and John Greenhurst was a local MP in 1422.

The Tudor Cafe

This building once adjoined the north side of the Talbot and these were evidence of early fragmentation of the burgages at the north-east side of the Causeway, onto what is now Market Square, as well as later encroachment westwards.

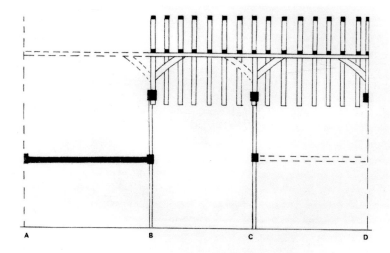

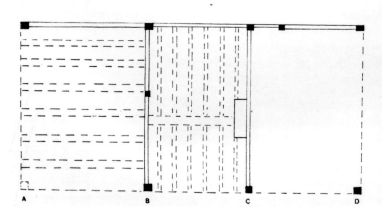

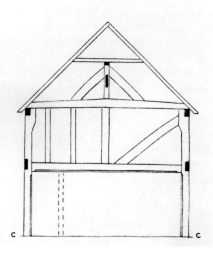

Plan of Greners – 26/27/28
West Street, Horsham.

Site of the Tudor Café.

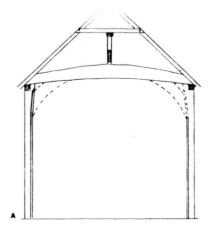

Drawings of
Tudor café plan.

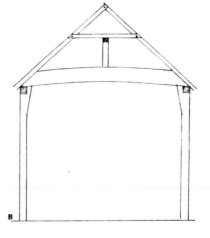

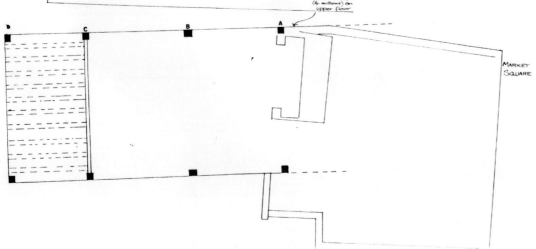

small window
(4 mullions) on
upper floor

MARKET
SQUARE

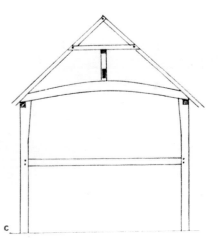

Horsham – 'Carfax' by Glyn Martin,
Cambrooke Fine Art Publishers Ltd.

These buildings, and eight of the others, were roofed with crown-posts, collars and central purlins, and that and the sooting evidence from open fires places them firmly in the fifteenth century, that is, before 1500. Remnants of the early structure of the **King's Head**, with painted timbers which were uncovered in the course of building work, suggest that this too may have been similar, or like the rear part of Palsheds (11 Causeway) which was a late open-hall with a side-purlin roof, that has been dendro-dated to 1513.

The King's Head, c.1890.

The King's Head, c.1910.

The King's Head, 1984.

The King's Head, 1912.

Causeway House: Horsham Museum by Sylvia Bright. A reconstruction of the probable appearance of the 'Tudor' front before it was plastered over in the 18th century.

Three of these buildings were aligned end-on to the street frontage, presumably because of the constraints of other ownerships or buildings (now gone); the rear range of Palsheds was an end-on addition to an earlier building, and it is likely that the rear range of the **Museum** was similarly end-on to a still earlier building, later replaced by the fine Elizabethan/Jacobean frontage.

Horsham Museum.

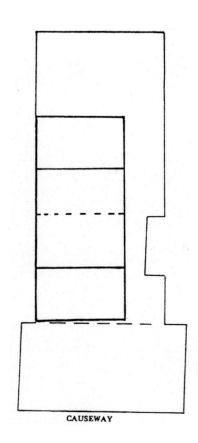

Enough of the crown-posted medieval core of this house can be traced to establish the outline of a four-bay hall house around which was constructed a most impressive late 16th/early 17th century framed-house, double-jettied at the front with oriel windows, which were replaced by bay windows in the 18th century.

CAUSEWAY

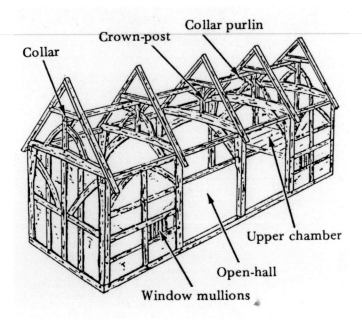

The four-bay timber-framed building which constitutes the core of the present building.

Causeway House, 1940.

Carfax Club, Horsham, 1912.

The same view in 1984. The only remaining medieval building on this burgage site (Heyborne's, late Bookers in 1611) is a five-bay hall-house whose end gable is concealed behind the 'John Gorman' front. The Central Market building was probably the 17th/18th-century inn called *The King of Prussia*, which probably included the earlier range.

Heybornes[10] (variously Bookers, Nyes or the King of Prussia) This building features in the 1611 survey, which supplies the most significant name for its early history.

*Richard Heybourne holds...one messuage, with a backside and garden adjoining **late Bookers** being half a burgage by the yearly rent (6d).*

The reference to Bookers makes it possible to trace the property from the mid-1500s in a sale to Heyborne of Rusper in 1588, who was cited for illegally cutting down trees on the land of the dissolved nunnery (at Rusper) in 1596. In this same year he and William Slater on adjoining property were involved in a *'greate controversy contention and stryfe'* with a neighbour, Henry Botting, over nuisance created by gutters and drains, which was resolved with a payment of 6d. Much subsequent history can be traced through the borough records. Timbers of the crown-posted early building can be seen on the northern wall of Pirie's Alley, and as there is another pre-1500 building on the south (see The Chequer), we know that alley is at least five hundred years old.

---

10 Bournes/Bornes; Heybournes/Heybornes: spelling was not standardized until the 19th century, therefore names of people and properties were often spelt in different ways – even within the same document!

A crown-post and brace from the first partition wall back from the Carfax.

Looking out of Skarfolkes (Carfax) up North Street, about 1620, by Sylvia Bright. The reconstructed appearances of the buildings are based on what remains of the Gaoler's House, *The King of Prussia*, and two buildings on the Chequer burgage.

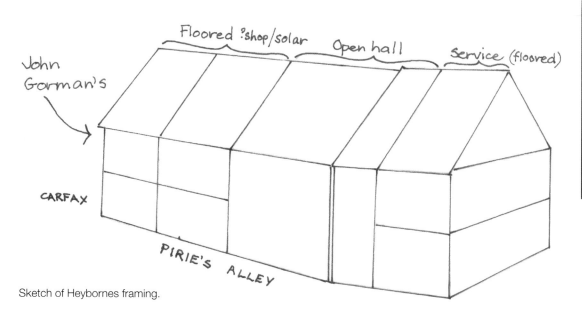

Sketch of Heybornes framing.

Much of the timber-framing of Heyborne's can be seen in the wall along Pirie's Alley, now filled with brickwork of several periods, where once was wattle-and-daub. The medieval rafter feet – thick and on the flat – are also easy to see under the eaves.

Looking down Talbot Lane or Pump Alley, one of Horsham's medieval passages. Buildings on each side are medieval in origin. The pattern of the timbers on the building centre background is of a queen-strut, side-purlin roof, built after 1550.

White Horse, south of Talbot Lane: about three bays of a pre-1520 building.

The soot-encrusted partition post that stands on the tie at A with original wattle-and-daub infill.

One end of the tie at B showing the jointing of the tie to the principal post, eave plate and rafter, and how the three-cornered brace or spandrel was pegged into the chamfered principal.

The Talbot

This is the most complete of the early buildings that have been identified flanking Pump Alley, all of which are (or were) crown-posted. The street frontage was originally aligned with the east end of the present entrance into Pump Alley. Heavy medieval joisting and a later chimney can be seen in the building that was the River Kwai restaurant, as well as wall-framing along the alley.

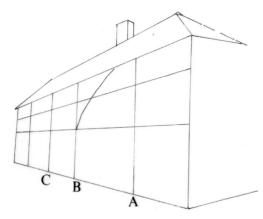

The probable bay divisions of the house above: the crown post over the open hall would have been at B and has been largely cut away by the inserted chimney. Much of the timbering has been replaced, but a characteristic curved brace remains.

The partition crown-post at C looking from the west.

Wall painting.

North of Talbot Lane on part of the burgage called variously the Star, or Wonder, or Talbot. A fairly complete hall-house of five bays.

Once an inn with the sign of a hunting dog (Talbot) it shared a yard with the **White Horse** to the south, where the timbers of a medieval cross-wing can be seen in the building at the rear of the kitchen shop. This has now been converted to apartments, and upstairs are the most complete wall-paintings in Horsham, no doubt dating from the late 16th or early 17th century when it was functioning as an inn. Evidence has been seen on the southern elevation of this wing for its earlier open hall, which would have extended south.

A probate inventory surviving for the White Horse in 1706 numbers twenty-four rooms, including a 'Club Roome'; by then, an extension had been added forward of the old frontage, with large windows and an attic, roofed with older timbers. A later inventory of 1729 still mentions the club room, as well as rooms decorated in blue, black and red, a 'boy on the Signpost' and 'Roley Poley pins and boule'.

Yerdleys, 17 Causeway. Courtesy of Rooney & Co estate agents.

Hadmans – 11, 12, 13 Causeway.

Yerdleys, 17 Causeway

The remnants of a three-bay crown-posted building survives within the front range of this house, butting up against no.16. Re-evaluation of the structure makes it most likely that this was a complete building with a two-bay hall and single floored end. Working from a deed of 1437, when a priest called William Yerdley was in occupation, it probably formed part of the endowment of the first private chantry in 1307/8 by Walter Burgeys, one of Horsham's first two MPs.[11] William was succeeded by John, described as a 'priest of noble birth, lord of Yerdley', who was granted permission for an altar (private chapel) in his house in 1470.

Subsequent owners/occupants included a widow from the Wicker family of Park House, a vicar of Horsham, Thomas Hutchinson (1742-69), and his widow and spinster daughters.

Hadmans also Palsheds, 11 & 12 Causeway

In the 1611 survey Henry Patching

> 'holds to him and his heirs of the Lord in free Burgage one messuage with a Backside and garden and one orchard.... being half a Burgage late Hadmans by the rent by the year (6d)'

The combination of a distinctive historical name, good dendrochronology and a run of deeds from the sixteenth century has made this one of the most rewarding houses to study in Horsham. It can be claimed that the earliest building surviving on the site (1481) was built for Richard Palshed, who was probably MP for Horsham at least once. The close-studded cross-wing at the south may have been original, but was more likely part of a fashionable 'up-dating' at the end of the 1400s. Palshed came from a family of lawyers who worked for the Dawtrey family and moved to Horsham from Elsted, probably to exploit its parliamentary status in order to further his career. From an assize record we know there was a Dawtrey house in Horsham in 1429. From the court records of Marlpost, It looks as though this was not the only property Palshed held in Horsham, but by 1500 he had moved on to Southampton where he became collector of customs, while keeping the Causeway property, which he enlarged (1513) and rented out, and although the family sold up in 1525, the house retained their name. Subsequently a fire in its rear range (1595/6) accelerated the process of 'modernisation' – which then involved building in a chimney and flooring over the open hall – and its position on a burgage plot meant the house was subsequently owned and tenanted by a sequence of notable Horsham families. Its relationship to adjacent properties north and south make it possible to work out how that part of the Causeway developed.

11   The Holy Trinity chantry by the north door of the church

The Chantry, Causeway

Outwardly an elegant eighteenth century building, this contains a three-bay crown-posted building with all the characteristics of a barn, although partially floored, which was not unusual. A recent examination claimed it to be a medieval house, but there are no signs of sooting from an open-fire. Documents suggest links with Butlers chantry, founded in 1447, with Flagstones which was once occupied by the parish clerk, and Hewells (Rectory) manor in 1734. In the early twentieth century it was home to Sir Hartley Shawcross, barrister and politician.

The Chantry, Causeway.

Horsham – 'The Causeway' by Glyn Martin, Cambrooke Fine Art Publishers Ltd.

A shop in Colletts Alley.

Crown-post in the fish and chip shop in Colletts Alley.

Glayshers in Middle Street was taken down and re-erected at the Weald and Downland Museum. This was one of 2 dolls (dating to around 1780) found along with a comb, teetotum and marbles, under the floorboards – why they were there is anyone's guess!

Evidence of sooting from an open hearth.

Colletts and Glayshers

The 'island' sites in the Carfax developed out of the zoning of market stalls, and the structure of surviving buildings north of Middle Street (Butchers Row) suggest that owners exploited both frontages. A 19th century drawing from the east shows an array of (probably) framed and jettied buildings.[12] The 'Horsham Shop', now at the Weald and Downland Open Air Museum stood on the site of the unappealing 1960s build, and was a rather specialised town building, with a narrow double-height open-hall at the rear of two shop premises, double-jettied. To its west is a building dated 1835, to the east Barclay's Bank, replacing the 'chemist' of the early drawing.

From 1754 the northern end of the buildings west of Colletts Alley were occupied by a baker and his family - the Champions, who were also millers – but in 1841 Jeremiah Collett was an assistant to James Waller, another miller/baker. The Colletts took over the business – Jeremiah and his wife, Mildred, had seven children – which they held until 1882. From then onwards the northern end was occupied variously by bakers, hairdressers, an umbrella maker and the Telephone Company. J.A. Wickersham occupied the northern end from 1889, sharing it with Day's fried fish in 1915. The southern end, on the corner of the alley, is still roofed with medieval sooted timbers, and was extended westwards at the end of the 1500s.

12   D. Hurst, History & Antiquities of Horsham, opp..p29 (1889)

The Chequer

This was the burgage site that extended between the two present-day access points to Pirie's Place, but the name has later become applied to the wealden at the northern end. There is also a remaining cross-wing from an even earlier house that occupied the site of the Stout House and its northern neighbour, which can be named as Durrants, from early photographs. The wealden still has the brackets for its end jetties, triangular mortices for the two-storey hall window, remains of its moulded dais beam, and heavy medieval joists in the southern end. The angled southern end wall shows that the Durrants cross-wing was already there when it was built.

The wealden was probably Thomas Smyth's *'howse called the Checker'* for which there is an inventory of 1631, and it was possibly his son, also Thomas, an innholder, who leased the property in 1663. A series of eighteenth century deeds in Arundel Castle shows the site was divided among at least five landlords and numerous tenants, including Sam Bryan the baker, who doubled as gaoler.

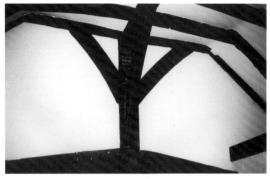

The crown-post that stood over the open hall of the wealden on the Chequer site in Horsham.

The door-head and remains of the moulded dais beam at the southern end of the hall of the Chequer wealden.

Wealden, south of Pirie's Alley. Shop divisions reflect the bay divisions of the original building. The gable window was inserted after the hall was floored over, and enlarged in the 19th century.

One of the crown-posts to the single-bay open hall.

Drawing of a wealden with a single-bay hall, as originally built.

18 & 19/20 Causeway

These two buildings were both built as small, three-bay wealdens. 18 now has a complete brick frontage, which its hipped roof is clearly raised at the eaves to accommodate, and framing is visible in the side walling. A building on the plot is first mentioned in 1425 when it was tenanted by a Simon Weylond, and working from this reference it seems likely that it was built on land belonging to the Holy Trinity chantry, so increasing the income of the endowment. By 1658 it was referred to as 'Mr Churcher's',[13] and later came into the hands of the Shelley family, who were landlords until 1889. William Pirie (headmaster of Collyer's) was briefly a tenant, as was the father of writer Hammond Innes who was born in Horsham.

19/20 was also built on chantry land but 'modernised' with weather-boarding, and by 1658 was divided into two as it is still, with a flying freehold. Its southern floored end was jettied around the corner with a 'dragon beam', a feature almost certainly intended to impress people walking into the town from the church. The moulded barge-board on its northern gable could indicate it pre-dates no.18, although not by much.

13   of Slinfold

Another three-bay open hall-house. Framing can be seen on the side walls between this and 19/20. Notice how the edges of the roof have been lifted, 'pagoda'-like, to accommodate the width of the brick front.

19/20 Causeway c.1895: close-studding and recessed hall still apparent, also jetty girder.

The dragon-beam to bear the joists for a jetty around a corner.

Original doorway into the open hall with its early doorhead. Note the rebate on the girder, top left, where it was supported for the overhanging jetty.

Site of Vigors, East Street looking west.

Vigors: decorative wind bracing.

Further wind bracing.

Braced collar within roof space.

Vigors

... Thomas Sheppard gent and Mary his wife, in right of her the said Mary... hold to them of the Lord in free burgage one messuage, one barn, one garden and one orchard... being a portion of a burgage...

This burgage plot originally ran east from the corner of Market Square, was fragmented into several ownerships before 1611 but named as The Star on the 1792 diagram. The eighteenth century burgages book contains an abstract of ownerships from 1681. Mary Sheppard was the daughter of Brian Voyce and Elizabeth Lyntott, both well-established Horsham families, suggesting the property was her inheritance.

The extensive medieval survival on the south side of East Street had not been fully identified when Horsham Houses was published in 1986. Extending along much of the south side of the street is a five-bay 'continuous-jetty' building with crown-post roof construction. This is one of three local examples of a characteristically urban type - a 'terrace' of small rentals. Attached to it, and apparently built at the same time, are three bays of a (four-bay?) high status wealden, with an unusual side-purlin roof construction, atypical in this area.

The first clues to possible reasons for this development are within a series of deeds held in Horsham Museum dating from 1566, relating to a property called 'Vigours'; a property with the same name was owned by Richard Fuller when he died in 1593. This distinctive name appears in much earlier local documents (late 1200s to first half 1300s), as the monk-bailiff of the estates of Fescamp Abbey in England. The Abbey had been gifted property in Sussex from before the Norman Conquest of 1066, and its English headquarters were at Steyning, where part of the parish church is a remnant of the Abbey's church. In this neighbourhood its properties were scattered throughout Horsham and neighbouring parishes, but for administrative purposes were bundled together under the heading of Shortsfield. It is reasonable to suppose that the bailiff needed an estate 'office' for his regular visits, and where better than Horsham.

That would explain both the high status and 'different' carpentry of the wealden, and the adjoining 'commercial lets' so beloved of ecclesiastical bodies, aimed at making a profit from a rented burgage plot.

East Street, looking East.

Netherledys.

Netherledys

This is actually outside the borough boundary and on the land that belonged to the Archbishop of Canterbury – Marlpost. It is a classic high-class wealden, built across the end of an earlier property, and until the gardens were developed, it was visible from the Worthing Road, an early way into the town. The earliest reference in the manorial court records is in 1472 when Edith Ryprose succeeded Henry to 'Nedeles'. Two years later William took over, to be succeeded by his widow Joan in 1487. A link to a property in the Causeway is flagged up in 1501 when Richard Palshud had become a tenant, and by 1523 his widow Joan had died 'holding a tenement and virgate of land called 'Nydeles' formerly William Rypcrofts [sic]'.

Crown-post on partition at south end of hall, above dais and screen.

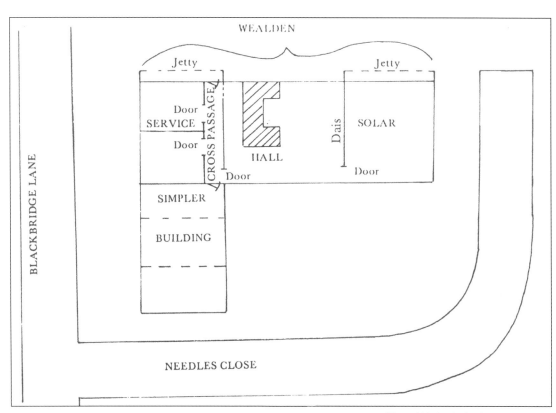

Corner assembly, south-west corner, showing principal post, end-tie, eave-plate and down-brace.

Plan of Netherledys house and site.

Crenellated dais beam above planked screen at south end of hall. The moulded girder (centre) and chamfered and stopped joists are all part of the inserted floor – late 16th/early 17th century. Notice original doorhead to the right.

Nos. 2 and 3 East Street in 1912.

2 and 3 East Street in 1984.

East Street north side
(Fawns, Stan's Way, Leach's aka Pizza Express)

... James Veraye and Dionisia his wife, one of the sisters and co-heires of John Jenner deceased, hold... one messuage with a backside, garden and two shops... being half a burgage...

This was the plot that had originally extended east from the northern corner of the present East Street, anchored on the Carfax by the Kings Head (Ask Italian). It stands out for the number of high status buildings we know were built before 1500, although not one is complete. There is clear evidence for three medieval open-hall houses, each with at least one cross-wing.

Fawn's was the most westerly, pictured in a **1912 trade magazine** with its stone roof, replaced by an unprepossessing modern building, which still contained some wall framing in the 1990s, and whose stepped frontage follows the ground plan of the early building.

Next came **Stan's Way**, where another cross-wing was identified just in time for its plan and sections to be included in 1986 – and now you can dine under its crown-post roof! It was only when it was dismantled for renovation that the evidence emerged to confirm that its hall had extended to the east, to be replaced by the Victorian building that now houses a charity shop.

Cross wing front, East Street.

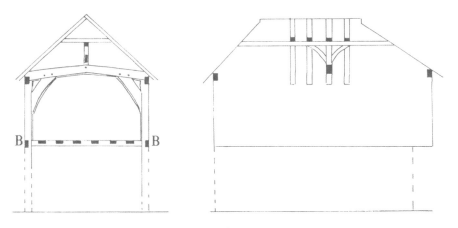

Plan and elevation of Leach Bros., no.4 East Street

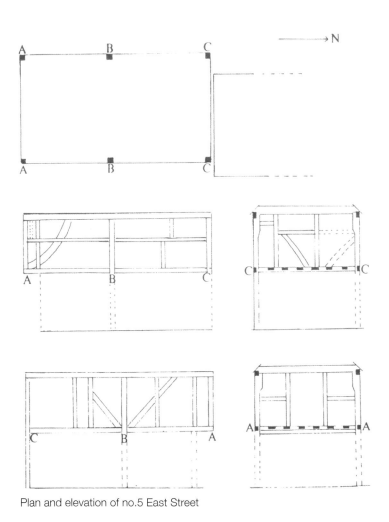

N →

Plan and elevation of no.5 East Street

The third building was once **Leach's** the fishmongers, and presently forms part of a pizza restaurant. Another early photograph shows that its hall also extended east, and must partially survive in a Chinese take-away. The cross-wing had the detail of a small first floor window that looked towards the west, and an upstairs 'en suite' garderobe to the rear. The range that extends to the west of the cross-wing and contains the rest of the pizza restaurant is an infill building of the 1600s.

21-23 East Street. Known for years as 'Leach's', after the fishmongers who occupied it. Jettied cross-wing to a hall house extending in the direction of the Chinese take-away, which may possibly contain some of the old roof.

An early view of the building shows the hall range, part of which may remain, and inserted chimney. The 19th-century building may have replaced another cross-wing.

Nationwide, Carfax & Bishops, Denne Road

...Thomas Rowland likewise holds one messuage, one barn, backside ad garden formerly Bishops and late Seales, being two burgages...

In 1986 these two buildings were linked as possibly being in the ownership of the same family: the Bishops. This name persists in the records of the Denne Road property for three hundred years, and Richard Bishop paid tax under Skarfolkes in 1524/5. Only the Denne Road property is in the 1611 burgage survey and indicated on the 1794 plan; the other is one of the 'illegal' developments on a Carfax 'island' but they were similar in plan. The evidence of the remains of the buildings – and old photographs and drawings – show that both originally consisted of a central open hall flanked by cross-wings.

Only the eastern cross-wing remains within Nationwide, and although its corner jetty is now buried within 18th century development, the 'giveaway' dragon beam can be seen above the entrance area. At the top of Denne Road the close-studding of the building's southern cross-wing makes a positive statement, and a drawing shows the whole building was treated in the same way, which would have been even more impressive. There is evidence for a garderobe at the rear of the southern cross-wing, and for contemporary door heads from the hall into the northern wing. The ownership/occupancy can be traced to 1911 when it housed The Beehive Inn, and was sold to a newsagent.

Nationwide in the Carfax, housing the eastern cross-wing.

Bishops, Denne Road.

A pen and wash drawing by CH Burstow,
1879, of the hall and cross wing.

The crown-post on the open truss above the upper chamber in the remaining cross-wing in what is now the Nationwide building society. Notice the high quality moulding of the cap and cushion of the crown-post, the deeply-gouged mould under the curved tie-beam, and the 'fillet' of wood that was between the two side-braces to the tie, which are now missing. In the background is the crown-post with down-braces marking the rear wall of the cross-wing.

Cowdens/Bottings

This building on its triangular plot is a good example of the complexities of trying to sort out a sequence of owners and/or occupants. For one thing, it is not the northernmost burgage; that distinction must be shared between the building that was Perry Place and whatever pre-dated Park House, once called Cockmans.

Firstly, what can the building tell us? Two-thirds is medieval but that immediately poses the question as to why the southern wing was rebuilt about 1600. The answer must lie in the fact that the roof timbers at the southern end of the central 'hall' are heavily charred, much more than even the heavy sooting from an open fire. This suggests that there was a southern cross-wing that was damaged or destroyed by fire. Structural details of the crown-posted 'hall' and northern cross-wing suggest it was built during the last quarter of the 1300s; it has similarities to the dated survival (1376) at the rear of 15, The Causeway, and also to the surviving cross-wing of Durrants, Carfax, adjacent to The Stout House.

In the survey made at the end of the 1700s there are **three** abstracts that relate to The George: Gowden or George, George Inn Briggs' part & George Inn Curtis' part. To this, can be added the Arundel Castle archives – again in **three** sets, as well as further surveys of 1809 and 1816 for the Duke of Norfolk.

1809 & 1816 refer to a *'messuage in North Street called the George Inn'* and *'heretofore the estate of John Wicker decd'*; Wicker was a master brewer who lived in Park House. This seems to have been 'Briggs part', which was *'Formerly in the tenure of Sarah Briggs'* but the recital of *'after Jas Beauchamp, Ann Briggs widow, Jn Goddard, Jas Beauchamp the younger & Ann Mitchell widow'* gives some idea of the sequence of occupancy.

'Curtis' part' must have been *'Another messuage called the George'* which was *'heretofore in the tenure of Rd Curtis, the elder, after Rd Cock'* but **'now united into one messuage,** late Edward Dubbins, surgeon, now Mrs Dubbins'.*

The later records show how the building was divided into more than one tenement. All these surveys were made to work out the number of parliamentary votes belonging to each property, and who could cast those votes (the landlord, NOT the tenant). The growing corruption of the parliamentary system, which brought about the illegal 'splitting' of burgage votes is dealt with in Albery's 'Parliamentary History of Horsham'.

The following illustrates the variety of sources that can be 'mined' for clues to the history of a building:

1327 tax[14] under Erlington	*Rd de Coudenne @ 1s 0¼*
1332 tax under Berwick	*Rd Coudenne @ 1s 6d*

Rd Coudene - *bailiff, MP (Horsham) 1379, 1397, 1399*
[variations Conden, Cowden]
(from The History of Parliament)

From 1370 Coudene acted as a feoffee of land at Wadhurst, Sussex, on behalf of Sir John Waleys of Glynde. He served as a juror at a coroner's inquest held at Mayfield in June 1377, and in the same capacity he provided evidence at the inquiries conducted at Horsham in 1395 and 1403, following the deaths of Sir Thomas Brewes [Sy MP] and Reynold, Lord Cobham of Sterborough, respectively. Up to March 1404 he was a trustee of land at Horsham belonging to William Rydelere I [MP 1381-97]. He is last recorded as witness to a deed at nearby Slinfold, in 1405.

This must be the man responsible for building the original North Street property, towards the end of the 1300s, establishing his rights as a burgess, and possibly to let.

1463 WSRO[15] Add Mss 39956 Grant [Warnham prop]
(a) John Roser sr. of Warnham
*(b) Richard Hayne, **John Bottyng sr.,**[16] Stephen Charman, John Roser jr. and Thomas Alysaunder*

1524 tax *SRS 56*	*North Street*	*John **Botting***

1544PRB[17]	*Jn Bottyng the elder, a 'bocher' (butcher)*
1548 PROB 11/32/17[18]	*Will of John Bottynge or Bottinge*
1551PRM[19]	*Hen Choll m Joan wid/o Jn Bottyng the elder*
1555	*Thos Broadbridge > Jn **Bottynge** in fee*

Messuage, barn, garden, orchard & 4acres pasture called Gowden

1587	*Hen Bottinge sr > Rd Gratwick & Rd White*
1588	*Conveyance on Heyburne's*

*ref. 'tenement sometimes **Jn Reed** now Hen **Botting** to North'*

---

14 Sussex Record Society vol 10
15 West Sussex Record Office
16 It is possible to compile some kind of Botting family tree from the parish registers, which start in 1544
17 Parish Register burial
18 In The National Archives
19 Parish register marriage

The George, formerly Bottings, after renovations in the 1970s. The northern wing was renovated in 1984.

1611 Survey (Horsham borough)

All that the aforesaid William SLATER the elder likewise holds one messuage with barns, backside, stables, garden, orchards and 4 acres land to the same adjoining with the appurtenances called the GEORGE late Bottings being two Burgages and a half Burgage by the rent 2s 6d

[This is marked on the 1794 diagram, showing that the whole plot was named the George, and extended roughly from Copnall Way to the present offices of the District Post, and contained more than one building. William Slater was the non-resident landlord who would have had tenants.]

1647 Rd Luckins (shoemaker & gaoler)	*as 1555 with 3 acres*
1653 Rd Luckins > Jn Young	*as 1555, occ Jn Hurst (turnkey)*
1653 Jn & Dorothy Young > Rd Yeates	*as 1555, occ Francis Hatcher*

From here on everything becomes more difficult until the 1840s onwards, when there is the tithe map and its apportionment, census returns (up to 1911) and local directories, which begin to relate to the map of the town before the developments of the 1970s and 80s.

Richard Coudene, whose name and career shows he moved from East Sussex to represent Horsham three times between 1379 and 1399, and as his name persisted, he is likely to have been responsible for the original North Street building. He can be added to the other MPs determined to place their stamp on the town – Richard Palshed of Hadmans, Thomas Bolter of no.15, and John Wantley, all in the Causeway.

Green Dragon, Bishopric, c.1920.

Minstrels & The Green Dragon
– aka The Olive Branch

Neither of these properties are on burgage sites, but both were built by ecclesiastical landlords and both have that prestigious double cross-wing plan. The quality of The Green Dragon is reflected in the decorative finish of its crown posts and details of its construction have been more visible since its refurbishment and rebranding. It was obviously of considerable status as would befit the house for the bailiff of Marlpost, where the manorial courts could be held. A more detailed investigation has been published in Horsham Heritage.

The Olive Branch, Bishopric, 2016 – originally The Green Dragon. Remains of timbering can still be seen in the side wall, and possible evidence for an underbuilt jetty. The tile-hanging now covers the rest of the upper floor timbering.

Originally two houses but now one: Minstrels, Causeway. The northern part is a characteristic Horsham hall-house with two cross-wings, each jettied at the front. The southern range was a continuous jetty house similar to some that used to be on the northern side of the Bishopric.

Minstrels is actually two buildings, the southern part being the commercial 'continuous jetty' much loved by ecclesiastical developers. Both parts were restored in the 1930s having been bought from the Church Commissioners, and it was given its present name. An account of the work done at that time told of the relocation of the fine stone hearth now on the ground floor from the room above – an important feature in the historic development of the house.

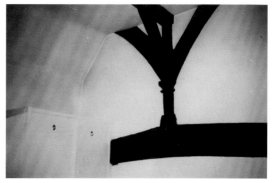

The carved and moulded crown-post standing on the tie that was originally over the open hall.

The northern side-wall of Minstrels' northern cross-wing, as revealed by work at no. 32, which shares this wall.

Horsham – 'The Causeway and St Mary's Church' by Glyn Martin, Cambrooke Fine Art Publishers Ltd.

Horsham – 'Cottages by the Church' by Glyn Martin, Cambrooke Fine Art Publishers Ltd.

Flagstones, Causeway, c.1990.

It was known to have been used as 'tied' homes for the parish clerk and sexton in the 19th century, although Flagstones was the clerk's house from c.1543 to 1626. Further research suggests it was among the endowments of the Holy Trinity chantry, and it was named as Wantleys in the 'chantry certificates' of 1543 when the tenant was a John Rose. The name 'Wantley' must be a memory of an earlier tenant, John Wantley, another of Horsham's MPs in the late 1300s, and it is probably his brass in Amberley church. That being so, there could be yet another link for there was a prolific Rose family in that parish.

Chapter Five
Horsham Types – A Summary

Wherever possible I have always tried to go back to an historical name for a building, preferably one that was in use for a reasonable length of time. Those in italics no longer exist. All the post medieval examples (PM) were built fully floored throughout and with integrated smoke control.

1. Simple open-hall house

The simplest form of timber-framed open hall house was a rectangle, made up of three units: a hall in the centre, of one or two bays, open from ground to rafters, flanked by the service and solar bays, each with a first floor room. In a town these could be built parallel with the street, or at right angles, and would serve as both residence and workplace for the owner. Later, when floors were inserted into the open halls, they would be sub-divided between tenants.

'Plain & simple' *Greners or Grenehurst (drawn by S. Bright)* West Street
                        Barkers, Carfax
                        Heybournes, Carfax, end-on
                        Kings Head, Carfax, (wall painting traces)
                        The Talbot (until recently, the River Kwai) Pump Alley, end-on
                        Tudor Cafe, Market Square (drawn by S. Bright)
                        Museum (rear) Causeway end-on
                        17, Causeway, Yerdleys
                        Hadmans also Palsheds, Causeway, rear end-on   DENDRO 1513
                                          (smoke bay/chimney   DENDRO 1595/6)

                        Chantry, Causeway, 18thC conversion of medieval barn
                        Colletts Alley x 2,'back-to-back'

Originally The King's Head, 2016.
Courtesy of Rooney & Co estate agents.

Carfax, 2016. Courtesy of Rooney & Co estate agents.

2. Wealdens; what is a wealden?

In estate agents' jargon, 'wealden' has become a term to describe almost any timber-framed house sited within the Weald of Kent, Sussex or Hampshire. For those who study buildings, the term applies to a specific type of building, best known and generally characterised by the house called Bayleaf, re-erected at the Weald and Downland Open Air Museum.

In its original form it is easily recognised. Like the standard open hall house, it has a central portion that is without a first floor, and this is flanked by floored ends. It has a single roof span, usually (but not always) hipped at each end, but what creates its distinctive appearance is that the upper level of the floored ends are jettied forward – they overhang the ground floor. As the building has a single roof, this meant that the length of eaves plate in front of the central hall needed extra brackets as supports, and a secondary eaves plate was set back. This gave the hall the appearance of being recessed.

The timetable of the development of this type is shrouded in the mists of time, but the earliest example known so far dates from c1340. It clearly appealed to the aesthetic eye over a long period, for it persisted for over 150 years, becoming adapted for different sites and needs. Many remaining examples are extremely elaborate, with the jetties extending round the ends of the floored bays, needing the diagonal girder called a **dragon beam**, the hall being recessed on both long elevations, and with all manner of decorative wall-framing. The plan was varied, just as with other houses, so that the hall could have one or two bays, and in some town situations the type was adapted to be built in 'terraces'.

As the type was first recognised in the south-east, it was called a *Wealden*, but as a result of much more thorough recording, examples of the type have now been recorded as far afield as Coventry and York.

When chimneys and first floors were introduced into the halls of wealdens, the flanking jetties were often underbuilt, and the recessed wall of the hall brought forward to stand flush, so that the characteristic appearance can be almost completely disguised. Often the bracing to what was the outer eaves plate can be the only remaining external clue.

Wealden   The Chequer, Carfax
                18, Causeway, Weylonds
                19/20, Causeway, Lewkens (+ corner jetty)
                Vigors, East Street (part)
                Netherledys *Marlpost*

3. 'Status' buildings

In the 1970s a superior style of timber-framed building was identified, whereby the service or solar bay (or both) was replaced with a wing at right-angles to the open hall, usually of two or more bays. R.T. Mason, one of the pioneers of studies of timber-framed buildings, wrote that *'the cross-winged house... stands in the upper vernacular stratum'* and that *'the occupant of a cross-wing house was clearly a man of some local importance'*. Because these wings were floored, they often survived when an open hall was demolished, and became incorporated into later houses. Sometimes surviving cross-wings can be the only evidence of the existence of the type. Judging from survivals and photographs, Horsham had an abundance of cross-winged houses, both with one (11) and two (6) wings.

Bournes – cross wing house with one wing – the side elevation view showing cross wing.

Side elevation of Bournes.

Bournes: front elevation – note the multi-flue chimney-stack.

The remains of Bournes' from the front: the chimney stack still remains as the roof begins to come off.

The collar purlin and crown posts of Bournes can be seen above the bonfire.

Crown post – Bournes.

Cross-wing	One	*Bournes*	Two	Nationwide (+ drawing)
		Fawns		Bishops (close-stud)
		Stan's Way		*Perry Place*
		Pizza Express		Cowdens/Bottings
		Butchers' Row		Minstrels Nth
		Palsheds, front DENDRO 1481		Green Dragon
		Flagstones		Nationwide (*Hall + i gone*)
		Durrants (Stout House)		
		Pump Alley Sth (wall-painting)		
		Rowlands, *Marlpost* (some colour traces)		
		15 Bolters (rear) DENDRO 1376		

Butchers Row/Middle Street – 1860s.

Fawns, East Street.

Perry Place, originally in North Street – a typical medieval house with central range and cross-wings.

Drawing of a shop in Butchers Row/Middle Street, by Sylvia Bright.

Durrants – Stout House.

Site of Durrants.

4. Continuous-jetty; a commercial exploitation

Probably more common than the wealden was the 'continuous-jetty' building. Although many were built at the same time as open-hall houses, these were always fully floored, and jettied on their long front elevation. They tended to be an urban type (there are numerous examples in York, some dating from the 1300s) as they could serve as 'terraces' of one-up-one-down artisans' dwellings and/or workshops. These were often exploitations of urban land by ecclesiastical bodies, and the three known examples in Horsham were all on such sites.

Continuous-jetty   Minstrels S (chantry)
(ecclesiastical)   Vigors (Fecamp) part
    Bishopric (Canterbury) terraces

5. Double jetty

Some town buildings were more specialist, with three floors, each jettied over the street; Horsham had one surviving early example, moved to the Open Air Museum at Singleton. A sixteenth century example survives close to the old Town Hall.

Double jetty
Glayshers, Middle Street (Weald and Downland Open Air Museum medieval double jetty)
11 Market Square (PM double jetty)

6. Dropped tie; more usable attic space

With the drive towards improvements such as controlled smoke and increased floor space, mostly during the period from 1500-1600, came a development called the 'dropped' or 'interrupted' tie. This increased the head-room in newly-available attic space, by doing away with the central part of the tie at the top of a truss and linking it with struts to a secondary tie, set lower down. An external clue can be when the heads of first floor windows are below the eaves level, at the level of the lowered attic floor.

Dropped-tie   Gaolers house
Causeway Lodge
Museum (front)
13, Causeway, 'Almshouses'

'Horsham – Causeway' by Glyn Martin, Cambrooke Fine Art Publishers Ltd.

Roof construction in 13 Causeway showing dropped tie.

Exterior, 13 Causeway.

7. 'Fashion' statements

Some details of timber-framed houses were clearly aimed at making an impression. Close-studding, where a series of vertical timbers or studs are used which are structurally unnecessary, suggested that the owner could afford to splash out on superfluous timber. Two local houses which had this feature have been dendro-dated – Bolters, in the Causeway (1500) and Parthings outside the town on Tower Hill (1479) – providing a range for the others. Jetties were a feature which may have developed from a structural device to gain room space at first floor (and above) on a restricted ground plot, and/or to prevent longer joists from 'bouncing'. They then seem to have become a 'display' feature, particularly when they were around a corner, or at more than one level.

Close-stud/jetty (Bishops)
 (Palsheds X wing)
 15 Bolters DENDRO 1500
 Red Lion
 Normandy

Gaolers House – now Crates in the Carfax. Courtesy of Rooney & Co estate agents.

Causeway Lodge, no.10 – a post-medieval timber-framed building with later rendering.

Bolters

Northchapel, North Street.

Close-up of Northchapel.

Harffeys, Carfax.

8. Other

Northchapel, North Street (medieval + much developed)
Turners, East Street (2-bay medieval fragment)
Harffeys[20], Carfax (inscription above door) PM[21]
Bishops/Turners (6 Causeway) PM
Andrew Robinsons (Denne Rd) PM
16 Bishopric & 17th terrace (Bishopric) PM
Kings Arms (Bishopric) PM

Inscription above the door, Harffeys.

20 In 1664, Thomas Harffey, 'apothecary' paid tax on 5 hearths at the building
    north of the King's Head – the date and name recorded above a doorway to
    a first floor room above a 'deli' (2016). When Harffey died in 1671, aged only
    39, he had fifty-two pieces of pewter as well as three pigs, ducks and poultry
    out the back, and left a widow with three small children. Both his son and
    grandson (also named Thomas) became apothecaries. In 1752, the grandson
    sold white mercury to Sarah Pledge, not knowing she was planning to poison
    James Whale, the husband of her fellow lodger at Corsletts. Sarah and her
    accomplice Ann Whale, were the last two convicted murderers to be burned
    at the stake on Broadbridge Heath common.

21 PM = post-medieval

Andrew Robinson's – Denne Road: Arun Lodge.

Arun Lodge, 2016.
Courtesy of Rooney & Co estate agents.

Brewmaster's house – 16/17 Bishopric.

The King's Arms, Bishopric, 2016.
Courtesy of Rooney & Co estate agents.

Some Conclusions

So what has the study of early buildings in Horsham been able to suggest about the town's pre-1600 development? I would pick out three things:

First: something about building sequences

Second: something about occupants during the first centuries of its existence

Third: something about the economy

At first, there does not seem to have been huge pressure on sites, as the important 'hall' of many buildings is parallel to the street frontage. There are exceptions – the group flanking Pump Alley and the island sites in the Carfax suggests that evidence may have been skewed by later development, particularly in the Victorian period. This possibility is strengthened by the number of 19th century dates on buildings in the centre, and close study of old photographs. The way in which the Wealden south of Pirie's Alley (The Chequer) was built in the mid-1400s to respect both the alley to the north, and the remnant of the cross-wing house to the south (Durrants), indicates that both were already established by the mid-1400s. Heybournes, north of the alley, also respects the line of the alley which must have been an existing boundary. Cross-wings were also a way of maximising site potential, and this must have been why several survived later re-development. It is worth noting that the then owners had the wherewithal to replace the halls, rather than converting them.

The only truly urban type (double jetty) to have been identified is now down at the Weald and Downland Open Air Museum (the Horsham 'shop'). Details of both that and the range along the west side of Colletts Alley suggests they were not isolated examples, and illustrate how the double frontages (north/south) were exploited and buildings compressed.

The number of cross-wing houses in medieval Horsham are an indication of an urban elite who could afford to make visible statements of their success, for a period spanning about 100 years from the end of the 1300s. These were generally on sites where they must have been replacements of earlier humbler dwellings, but the lack of much in the way of recycled elements suggests there were plentiful supplies of building timber and residents who could afford to invest. This elite must have been resident, their houses serving as combined dwelling, workshop and business premises.

Pencil drawing of Causeway, Horsham looking towards St. Mary's parish church; unsigned.

In the absence of a comprehensive campaign of dendro-dating, some idea of the chronological sequences of development is limited to looking at abutments of buildings, like the Chequer. Dendro dates on two Causeway houses have illustrated how important they can be in establishing who might have been responsible for each of several phases, and has raised the interesting question of how soon new styles 'caught on'. Bolters (no.15) was fully floored, jettied along both long elevations, close-studded and built with a brick chimney, and dating shows it was built soon after 1500. It must have replaced an earlier open hall house, of which a small cross-wing survives at the rear (dated 1376). About thirteen years later, when an addition was made at right-angles to the rear of Palshuds (no.11) although it did have the more 'modern' side-purlin roof, and possibly a smoke hood, it was still built with an open hall. The masonry chimney stack was not built until about 1595, and then a house fire was the stimulus!

A working knowledge of the documentary background has made it possible to suggest a rationale behind surviving continuous jetty buildings – all on ecclesiastically owned sites – and 'stand-out' buildings like the west end of Vigors in East street – probably on a site leased to the Abbey of Fescamp's Shortsfield Manor. Surviving documentary evidence also illustrates the importance of the parliamentary status of the town in attracting ambitious (and ultimately wealthy) immigrants, seeing such office as a stepping stone and enabling Horsham's 'movers and shakers' to develop a cosmopolitan outlook, which fed into the built environment.

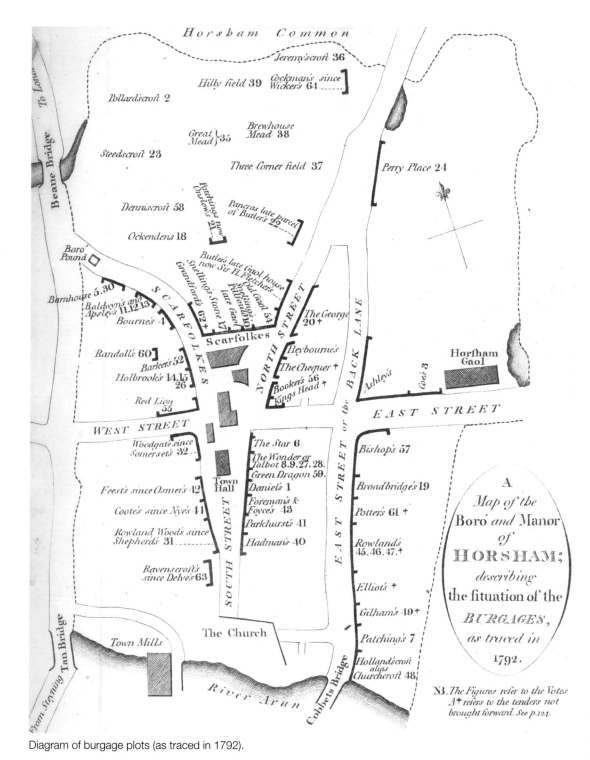

Diagram of burgage plots (as traced in 1792).

Appendix

Approximate numbers of historic buildings

136 in historic Horsham parish
    (inc Roffey, Southwater, BBH, N Heath)
62 Town (some doubles)
    further 10 demolished before 1972
13 in Causeway

Note on Burgage holdings in Horsham

Horsham was first recorded as a borough in 1235, when the town was required to provide a jury, and circumstantial information indicates it was probably granted this status at the beginning of the 1200s. The town was a 'burgage tenure' borough, which meant that the right to vote – both in matters of local administration and parliamentary representation – went with the *ownership of a burgage plot*, whether it had buildings on it or not. This did not prevent influential residents acquiring more than one plot, and then developing them and sub-letting, and printed taxation lists suggest this was happening by the end of the 1200s and into the 1300s.

The 52 original burgage plots, each rented at 1s. a year, seem to have remained intact until c1439, but as parliamentary representation became increasingly important, this led to sub-division not only of plots, but of votes, and by 1502 there were 57 for 52s 6d. Apart from 39 whole burgages, the first surviving written survey (1611) lists 17 halves and 17 'portions'. In 1764 a written survey made by Lord Irwin's gardener, which listed 66 properties (including fields and parts of houses) and about 85 votes, shows just how fragmented (and corrupt) the original scheme had become. The diagram of *'the situation of burgages'* that is widely printed was not drawn up until 1792, and was intended to settle a voting controversy; the numbered list that went with it has not been found.

From studying written records and comparing these with the maps of the town that exist from the 19th century onwards it is clear that the original plots were roughly rectangular, generally extending back from a narrow frontage on the market area to the north/south trackways east and west of the town. Those burgages that became divided earliest seem to be those that lay along each side of the tracks that became East and West Street, and early references also show that the name 'East Street' was given at first to the line of Denne Road/Park Street [Place] – which was also called Back Lane, Friday Street and Shitbourne Lane.

As the owner/occupiers of burgage plots were likely have been the wealthiest and most influential residents, and with the added bonus of two parliamentary votes became increasingly important, these are the most promising sites to investigate for early houses. Focused on the heart of the town – the market place, Skarfolkes or Carfax – they also present some of the best examples of continuing development and adaptation.

The borough eventually came into the hands of the Duke of Norfolk, and many relevant records are held at Arundel, so one might think that it would be easy to unravel the history of individual burgages by consulting surveys made in 1809, 1811 and 1816. It is certainly possible to glean quite a lot of information, but just one catalogue entry relating to properties lying east of the old Town Hall will illustrate some of the difficulties:

Several messuages backsides barns buildings, gardens and other premises now in the several tenures of Thomas Lintott Sarah Ridge, Daniel Roberts and John Dale, formerly part of the Wonder or Talbot inn being the great parlour and the vaults and cellars under the same and half the great chamber over the said great parlour, next adjoining to the Star inn, and the moiety of the garrets of the new buildings fronting the Market Place, and all the buildings, gardens or enclosed grounds on the N side of the way leading from Friday Lane [Denne Road] through the Wonder inn to the Market Place [Pump Alley] with a piece of ground on the N side of the said way, and the uppermost house of office on the S side of the yard of the Wonder and one moiety of the barns, stables, yard or yards, ways or waste places as the same were formerly set out and bounded by pegs and otherwise, and also the joint and free use of the said way or passage and the pond adjoining to the said way; piece of ground, being the E end of an orchard formerly of the estate of John Chasemore and belonging to the Wonder or Talbot inn and formerly part of the garden or orchard adjoining the dwelling house occupied by Philip Humphreys and which is burgage land held at the yearly rent of 3d...

East Street, c.1890

Note on Dendro-chronology

The science of dating timbers by counting growth rings has developed considerably over the past decades. When suitable samples can be taken, which should include heart to sapwood edge, it can provide very precise felling dates, and we know timber was used for construction within no more than 2 years. Unfortunately, the skills of timber-management were well developed in Sussex by an early date, and allied with a highly suitable climate, much timber suitable for building could be felled before laying down sufficient growth rings for current sampling procedures. Nevertheless, dated examples are being accumulated slowly, and when set against documentary information, are giving valuable points of reference. Three of the four earliest buildings identified in West Sussex have been dated (in Rudgwick, Horsham North Heath and Duncton) as well as properties in Horsham town, along with examples in Steyning, Shoreham, Poling, Clapham and Heyshott.

Chesworth

Historically Chesworth is probably the most important site in Horsham, the name believed to derive from Ceoldred's worth – the farm or homestead belonging to Ceoldred. He must have been an Anglo-Saxon of some clout that his name has persisted for centuries, albeit in a mangled form. Possibly he had the status of a thegn – a wealthy landowner. The site is just along the river from the parish church, and both are close to an early river crossing, so it is tempting to see a connection between the two. What is certain is

Watercolour painting of the interior of St Mary's Parish Church, Horsham. This shows the De Braose monument in the mid-ground with the figure of a knight on top.

Chesworth – surviving timber framing within building

Chesworth – rear

Chesworth – remains of brick range

that the de Braose family, who were tenants-in-chief of the Rape of Bramber, probably funded the first stone church and were crucial in establishing Horsham's borough status, can be linked to the site for several hundred years; the last in the direct line was buried in 1395, beneath his effigy in the parish church. During their ownership both Edward I and Edward II were guests at the house, which must have functioned as the 'manor house' of Horsham.

By the sixteenth century the property had passed through a female heir to the Howard Dukes of Norfolk, and the remnants of the significant courtyard house that they built can still be traced in the present building on the site, although it has been heavily over-restored. Most notable are the remains of the brick-built Earl of Surrey's 'tower'; early local histories mistakenly called this a chapel. Although a private family chapel was known of, it was almost certainly more of a dedicated room, than a large edifice.

Chesworth was to feature in the shenanigans of the Howard family during the reign of Henry VIII, as Catherine Howard spent time there as an adolescent. A detailed study of the house and its history was published by the Museum Society in 1998.

Some Horsham notables

(cf History of Parliament on-line; but 1422-1504 still in progress)
Albery lists to 1478 and from 1529, but notes that '1482-1523 returns have not been found'.

Bolter

Probably the son of William, Thomas Bolter (MP 1402 & '07) and his wife Alice conveyed to William Seeke, chaplain, a plot of land at Horsham containing an intriguing *'acquaecadium scilicet waterfall'* in 1411. Reference to more land and a house belonging to Bolter was made in another deed, dated 1425. By 1447 his widow Joan had acquired a life interest in a tenement and garden in the town, which was to revert after her death to William Bolter, probably Thomas's son. 15 The Causeway was named as 'Bolters' into the seventeenth century, and a small part at the rear of the present house was built soon after 1376.

Butler or Boteler family

The 1611 burgage survey records the corner site of Carfax onto North Way (Street) as *'a certain house called the gaol house... with twenty acres... called **Butlers**, sometime the gaol house being 5 burgages and a half...'.*

Galfrid (Geoffrey) paid tax as a burgess in 1296 and John in 1327 and 1332; the latter was one of Horsham's two MPs at four parliaments between 1322 and 1344, and was involved in a land purchase at Itchingfield in 1343. John was the wealthiest man living in Horsham in both 1327 and 1332, witnessing deeds in the town from 1380 to about 1409.

In 1419 Henry, very probably John's son, was one of several (trustees) who settled rents on Margaret Brewes, and he was MP for Horsham five times between 1386 and 1398. In June 1398, after representing the borough in Parliament for the last time, Boteler procured a royal pardon, perhaps because of the precarious political circumstances of the time. There can be little doubt of his loyalty to Richard II, for 18 months later, on 23 Jan. 1400, he was to be arrested and brought along with Sir William Burcester and Sir Thomas Sackville II before Henry IV's council, as having been involved in a recently failed plot to dethrone the King and restore his predecessor. Burcester had personal links with Thomas, Lord Despenser, a principal mover in the conspiracy, and perhaps Boteler had followed his lead in lending Despenser support. Whatever the facts of the matter he and his fellows were discharged on bail, on the surety of Sir Robert Denny and others, after just five days in custody, and were presumably found innocent when brought to trial. Their shared experience brought members of the group closer together: in September following Burcester made Boteler a feoffee of his estates, together with Sackville and another of those arrested in their company; just a few weeks later, Sir William acted as a witness when Boteler was enfeoffed by John, son of Hugh Hasell of Arundel, of land at Broadwater and Sompting, near the Sussex coast. The connection between the families of Burcester and Boteler was to continue for several years longer.

Henry's son, also Henry, succeeded his father to become an MP on five occasions between 1413 and 1427. By September 1410 Boteler junior was in possession of a field at Horsham known as 'Boteleresmede'; two years later he acquired a dovecote in the garden of a house at Lynde, [an early crossroads of the Worthing Road and Bishopric] in the same parish; and over the years he came to hold a number of other properties in the vicinity, including land at Roffey called 'Elyottes', 'Cokhuntys Grove', 'Hethelond' and 'Segrymes'. Boteler witnessed deeds at Horsham as late as 1432.

While attending the shire court at Chichester for the elections to the Parliament of November 1414, Boteler attested the indenture of return for the knights of the shire. Like his older namesake and presumed father, he became involved in the affairs of Sir William Burcester. By a transaction completed in 1421 he was made a co-feoffee with Walter Urry (Burcester's son-in-law) and Richard Wakehurst of lands in Warnham, by grant of Burcester's widow Margaret. He and Urry had been colleagues in the Parliament of March 1416 and were to be associated on other occasions, too.

The date of Boteler's death is not known, but it must have happened before September 1436, for it was then that the trustees of his lands handed them over to another group, headed by Wakehurst and Urry, which proceeded to found a chantry known henceforth as 'Boteler's chantry' in Horsham church. There, prayers were to be said for the welfare of the King and Horsham's lord, John, duke of Norfolk, and for the souls of Boteler and his wife Mary in the illustrious company of Henry IV, Henry V, Queen Katherine and the previous duke. Royal licence was obtained in July 1444 for the endowment of the chantry with property at Horsham and Itchingfield worth £7 a year. Further details of its endowment in lands and rents can be found in the records of 1535, made before the dissolution of chantries (Sussex Record Society vol 36).

Alfred Berwick
(decd after 1541)
b. by 1486. m. by 1509, Agnes, daughter of Thomas Bradbridge of Horsham, 1 daughter

He was almost certainly from a local family which had members living in Arundel, Pulborough, Steyning and elsewhere in Sussex.

Berwick was to make his career in the service of the house of Howard. The **first sure glimpse of him, in 1507,** is as a feoffee of the East Anglian estates of Thomas Howard, Earl of Surrey: six years later he appears on a list of the family's servants as the surveyor of its manor of Reigate in Surrey and as the recipient of a fee of 10 marks. In 1509 the manor of Legh in Cuckfield, Sussex, had been settled upon Berwick and his wife: their title proved uncertain, but an action in the courts went in their favour, although by 1540 the manor had passed into the possession of others. **In 1517 Berwick's wife received a life interest in the manor of Denne in Horsham**. The borough, part of the Howard patrimony, was held by Agnes, dowager Duchess of Norfolk, who kept her household there through much of Henry VIII's reign. Berwick was the most substantial inhabitant of Horsham in 1524 [in the Causeway] when he was assessed at £54 6s.8d. in lands and fees by the subsidy commission, of which he was himself a member: the commissioners added a note that his income had fallen since his contribution to the loan of 1523 because he had parted with his comptrollership of the customs at Chichester to Thomas Alcock, and had transferred some lands to his 'daughter-in-law' (really his brother-in-law's daughter) Eleanor Hussey.

As a leading figure in Horsham and a servant of the Duke of Norfolk, Berwick was an obvious choice as **one of the town's Members in 1529**. A Thomas Berwick, perhaps an ancestor, sat for Horsham in the Parliament of 1442. It is possible that Alfred Berwick already had experience of the House: **the borough's returns to the early Parliaments of Henry VIII's reign are lost,** but the same considerations as applied in 1529 would have done so between 1510 and 1523 and Berwick's inclusion in the subsidy commission between 1512 and 1515 points in the same direction. Both he and his fellow-Member and kinsman Henry Hussey presumably sat again in 1536, when the King asked for the re-election of the previous Members. Either or both may have sat in the following Parliament, that of 1539, for which the names of Horsham's representatives are not known, and possibly also in 1542.

Berwick's family was involved in the downfall of Queen Catherine Howard. During her trial in 1541 stories were related of her youth at Horsham and Lambeth, and of her relationship with Henry Mannock, her music teacher. Several of the ladies attending on the duchess had carried messages between Catherine and Mannock, and one of these was **Berwick's daughter, Dorothy**, whose evidence on the betrothal between Catherine and Mannock threatened the validity of the King's marriage. There is no indication that either Berwick or his daughter suffered for these indiscretions, but a similar silence shrouds the rest of Berwick's life and the time of his death. He may have been the 'Averyce' Berwick who in 1545 delivered £300 to Anthony Aucher for timber for ships and storehouses at Boulogne, or even the Alfred Berwick who 11 years later obtained, with his wife Joan, a rent charge out of the fee-farm of Canterbury, Kent.

Richard Palshud

The curious name of Palshud originated as a place-name north of Petworth, but had become a personal name by the thirteenth century, for a family of Wealden tenants of the Archbishop of Canterbury, who clawed their way up the social scale through the law, until *'Richard Palshyd als Palshud of Southampton, late of London, Elsted[22] and Horsham'* is described as 'gent' and 'attorney' in a public record of 1500[23]. It was either this man or more probably his father who was appointed as attorney on some Petworth property belonging to Andrew Dawtrey in 1450[24], and we know from the 1429 indictment of Roger Elyot, chapman & MP, for burglary and rape, that the Dawtrey family had a foothold in Horsham. These references establishes the link between Palshud and the Dawtreys, and a connection to Horsham and its parliamentary potential, which presumably he then exploited, building a new house on a burgage plot in 1481 and moving on to the lucrative post at Southampton. The long-standing connection to Canterbury property in the Weald may also have been brought into play, given that Palshud was also a Marlpost tenant.

The dendro date for the second build on the burgage site in the Causeway suggests that Palshed retained the property as a 'cash cow' and that it was his son who sold up after his father died in 1523.

---

22 NW Sussex, adjacent to Harting.
23 Cal.Pat.Rolls Hen VII pt II 1494-1500, p205, M15
24 1449/50 WSRO AddMss 12320

Bibliography

Local

Sussex Archaeological Society – various vols
Sussex Notes & Queries – various vols.
Sussex Record Society – especially vols 2, 3, 7, 10, 14, 21, 23, 36, 42 (2), 91
Albery, W. A. *Parliamentary History of Horsham 1295-1885*
   (1926, Longmans)
Millenium of Facts: Horsham & Sussex (1947 Horsham Museum Society)
Booker, J.M.L. (ed) *The Wiston Archives* (1975)
Chatwin, D. *The Development of Timber-framed Buildings*
   in the Sussex Weald (1996, Rudgwick Preservation Society)
Elwes, D.G.C. *The Family of de Braose 1066-1326* (Exeter, 1883)
Hudson, T.P. *A History of Horsham*
   (Victoria County History Vol VI pt 2 1986; reprint 1988)
Hughes, A.F. *Chesworth: The Story of a Local House*
   (1998, Horsham Museum Society)
Horsham Heritage articles:
   1   (2000) The Red Lion
   4   (2001) County Gaols (1)
   5   (2002) County Gaols (2)
   7   (2002) Time to reconsider (Palshuds)
   13 (2005) East Street
   15 (2006) The Vicarage
   16 (2007) Poor Relief
   18 (2009) Inns of Market Square
   19 (2010) Green Dragon
   20 (2011) Erosion of Marketplaces
   21 (2012) The Anchor
   22 (2014) More about Palshuds
   23 (2015) 15th century almshouses

Hurst, D. *History and Antiquities of Horsham* (2nd edition 1889, Lewes)
Salzman, L. *The Chartulary of Sele Priory* (1923)
Steer F.W. (ed) Arundel Castle Archives, Vol 1 (1968) Vol 2 (1972)
Willson, A.N. *A History of Collyer's School,* 1532-1964 (1965)

General

Alcock, Barley, Dixon, Meeson. *Recording Timber-Framed Buildings:*
   an illustrated glossary (1996 CBA)
Bailey M. *The English Manor c1200-c1500* (2002, Manchester UP)
Birch R. *Sussex Stones: the story of Horsham Stone and Sussex Marble*
   (2006, Horsham)
Brown R.J. *Timber-Framed Buildings of England* (1990, Hale)
Brunskill R.W. *Traditional Buildings of England* (1992, Gollancz)
Brunskill R.W. *Brick Building in Britain* (1990, Gollancz)
Cleere H. & Crossley D. *The Iron Industry of the Weald*
   (1985, Leicester UP)
Clifton-Taylor A. *The Pattern of English Building* (1980, Faber & Faber)
Harris R. *Discovering Timber-Framed Buildings* (1993, Shire Books)
Lander, H. *House and Cottage Interiors* (1982, Acanthus Books)
Mason, R. *Framed Buildings of the Weald*, 2nd ed. (Coach, 1969)
Reynolds, S. *An Introduction to the History of English Medieval Towns*
   (OUP 1977)

Houses by Street

Key:

B	= burgage plot or part;
W	= wealden;
X or XX	= cross-wing 1 or 2;
JJ	= cont.jetty

The sites of original buildings which no longer exist are in italics.

1686 Burgage Survey

Skarfolkes	Red Lion B	Waterstones	Wm Griffith, Ann & Judeth
	Between the Lines B		Nye lt Sherleys
	Barkers B	Lintotts family home	*Rd King sr*
	Bournes B X	*demolished*	Rd Lintott (Goulde)
	Grandfords B	Coroners	
	Butlers B	Gaoler's house	

'Islands'	Nationwide XX		
	Colletts Alley		
	Glayshers		
	Laura Ashley		

East Street	*Fawns X*	Bath Store	
	Stan's Way X	Bishops XX	
	Pizza Express X	Vigors JJ W	

North Street	Kings Head B	Ask	Art Rowland lt Thos Michell
	Harffeys B	Carmella's Deli	Geo lt Jn Booker
	Durrants & Stout House B X		
	The Chequer B W	Wealden	Wm Weller lt Thos Sneller
	Heybornes	King of Prussia	(& Rd Weller)
	The George	Cowdens/Bottings XX	Rd Curtis lt Yates
	Cockmans	Park House	Jn Wicker was Nich Sturt;
	Northchapel		Jn Picke lt Wick.

South Street (East)	The Star B The Wonder or Talbot B White Horse B Formerly Bishops lt Turners B Causeway House B Parkhurst B Hadmans als Palsheds B X		Phil Chasemore lt Nic Sheppards Jn & Joan Michell lt Wheatleys Ben Terry fmly Potters since B lt T Wm Coe fmly Foremans/Foyces
South Street (West)	Ravenscrofts B *Woodgates/Somersetts B*	*Grenehurst B*	*Jn Somersell fmly Allens since father*
Rectory Manor etc	13/A Seghere/'almshouses' 15/16 Bolters 17 Yerdleys 18 Weylonds W 19/20 Lewkens W Flagstones X Chantry (barn) Minstrels I & II XX & JJ	*(Smith map)*	
East Street (Denne Rd)	Late Andrew Robinson B Bishops lt Seales B XX *Ashleys viz Wist 1457* *Perry Place XX*		Art Rowland *Nic Best* *Gardiner lt Mt White*
Bishopric	Green Dragon XX Brewmasters (King and Barnes) 17thC cottages Med terrace *demolished JJ* Kings Arms Rowlands Netherledys W		

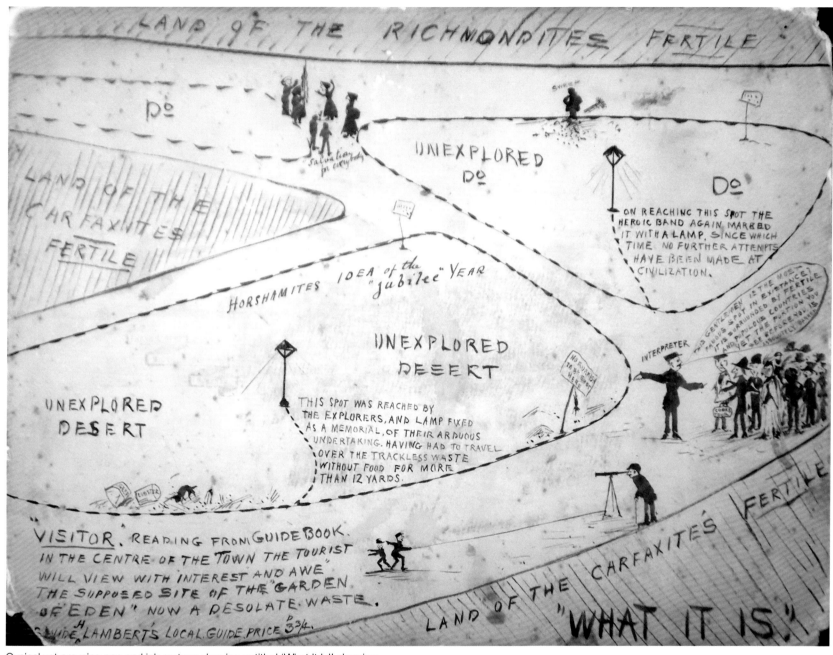

Cynical yet amusing pen and ink cartoon drawing entitled 'What It Is!' showing
a crude road layout of Carfax, Horsham (1887), thought to be by F Burstow.

Index of People & Places

List of Illustrations

Every attempt has been made to find the Copyright holder of certain images. If you are aware of the Copyright holder, please let us know so that we can amend this in future editions of this book.

About the Author

Dr Annabelle Hughes' own personal story is as fascinating as some of the backstories of the houses she so enthusiastically writes about. She lived in Malaysia and Australia during her formative years before moving to England, and eventually to Horsham in 1970. It was when she became involved with the Horsham Society in a campaign to save Horsham's Prewetts Mill from demolition that she began to cultivate what would become a lifelong interest in timber-framed houses and their captivating stories. Whilst raising four children, she completed an Open University honours degree and then embarked on further study, completing an MA in History at Sussex University. Her involvement with the Wealden Buildings Study Group led to her pursuing a Doctorate: her chosen subject, timber-framed buildings, led to widespread amusement and many a raised eyebrow among her lecturers at the time! Undeterred, and in keeping with her off-the beaten-track approach to life, she spent six years knocking on the doors of old properties, asking the bemused owners if she could scramble on her hands and knees through their roof spaces: she continues just as enthusiastically today to tell the stories of the buildings of Horsham and the people who lived in them. Having previously served as secretary, newsletter editor and chairman, Dr Annabelle Hughes continues as the President of the Horsham Society and is also a trustee of Horsham Museum Society and long-time Friend of Horsham Museum.

Publications

PhD: *The evolution and ownership of timber-framed houses within the old parish and market catchment area of Horsham* (1988) by Annabelle F. Hughes

Sussex Clergy Inventories, 1600 – 1750 (Sussex Record Society) (2009) by Annabelle Hughes

The 1844 Tithe Map of Horsham Parish: Parts 1 & 2 of Horsham (Northern Part) – Covering Roffey, Littlehaven, North (2005) by Alan Siney and Annabelle Hughes

Henfield: some history and an inventory of its most historic buildings (2004) by Annabelle Hughes

The 1844 Tithe Map of Horsham: Parts 3, 4 and 5 of Horsham Parish Covering Southwater and Broadbridge Heath (2002) by Alan Siney and Annabelle Hughes

Amberley Castle 1103 – 2003: A Celebration of 900 Years (2002) by David Arscott and Annabelle Hughes

West Sussex Barns and Farm Buildings (2002) by Annabelle Hughes and David Johnston

Sussex Depicted: Views and Descriptions 1600 – 1800 (2001) John H. Farrant (Annabelle Hughes, contributor)

The Shelleys of Field Place: The Story of the Family and Their Estates (2000) by Jeremy Knight and Annabelle Hughes

An Historical Atlas of Sussex (1999), published by Phillimore & Co. Ltd. (Annabelle Hughes, contributor)

Hills: Horsham's Lost Stately Home and Garden (1999) by Annabelle Hughes and Jeremy Knight

No More Twist: inventories of Horsham tradesmen 1612 – 1741 (1999) by Annabelle Hughes

Best Foot Forward: inventories of Horsham shoemakers 1626 – 1734 (1999) by Annabelle Hughes

Clothying oft maketh Man: inventories of Horsham tradesmen 1626 – 1734 (1999) by Annabelle Hughes

Chesworth – Horsham: The Story of a Local House, Once the Focus of a Royal Scandal (1998) by Annabelle Hughes

Pen, Ink and Scalpel: inventories of Horsham professionals 1626 – 1750 (1998) by Annabelle Hughes

Hell for Leather: tanners and tanning in Horsham 1520 – 1741 (1998) by Annabelle Hughes

The King's Head (1998) by Annabelle Hughes

Down at the Old Bull and Bush: inventories of Horsham Innkeepers 1611 – 1806 (1997) by Annabelle Hughes

Chennelsbrook Farm (1997) by Annabelle Hughes

Hammer and Chisel: inventories of some Horsham tradesmen 1614 – 1740 (1996) by Annabelle Hughes

Seven Horsham Houses: a brief account of some of Horsham's historic buildings and the families who lived in them (1996) by Annabelle Hughes

Husbands & Widows: Goods & chattels of some Horsham families 1614 – 1740 (1995) by Annabelle Hughes

Head to Toe: Goods & chattels of some Horsham tradesmen 1612 – 1734 (1995) by Annabelle Hughes

The Archbishop's Palace, West Tarring (1987) by Annabelle Hughes

Horsham Houses (1986) by Annabelle Hughes

Bygone Horsham (1982) by Anthony Windrum and Annabelle Hughes

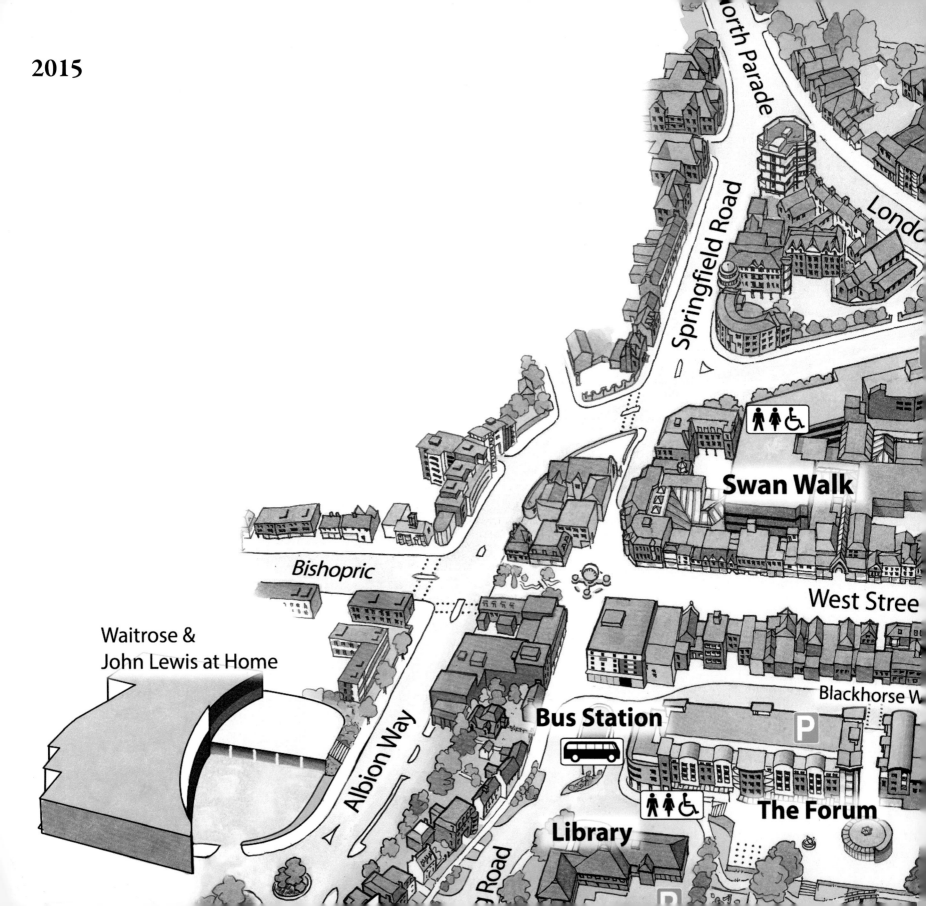

2015

North Parade

Springfield Road

London

Swan Walk

West Stree

Bishopric

Waitrose &
John Lewis at Home

Blackhorse W

Albion Way

Bus Station

P

The Forum

Library